D0797060

SPEAK
WITH CONFIDENCE

SELL
WITH AUTHORITY

ADVANCED PRAISE

I have had 40,000 people go through my courses and programs. Jane M Powers' wit and humor, her ability to command a room, and her ability to sell in an aligned and powerful way inspired me to hire her to help me craft the opening of my talk, tighten my message, and sell in an aligned manner in 90 minutes or less. Over the span of six months, I went from converting 5K in a presentation to my personal best of $128,000 in 75 minutes!

—Jay Fiset, Founder, Mastermind to Millions

Ignore this book at your own risk. It's a must-read for anyone who's serious about creating and delivering an impactful message that sells . . . while having fun doing it.

**—Isabelle Mercier, Brand & Business Performance Catalyst,
TEDx Speaker, One of North America's
Top Small Business Influencers**

Jane M Powers is the go-to person for speakers who want to sell successfully and with high integrity. If you want to master how to engage any audience and boost your bottom line, *Speak with Confidence. Sell with Authority* is a must read. There are no meaningless platitudes in Jane's book—only proven methods of success to turn your message into money.

**—Iman Aghay, Founder and Director, Success Road Academy®,
Founder, Entrepreneurs International Network™**

I'm a professional performer who's been on stage my entire life. As soon as I met Jane, I knew I needed to work with her. Together, we transformed my talk in one day. I felt so grounded and powerful that I was able to communicate exactly the message I wanted to my audience.

—Molly Mahoney, Camera Confidence Coach, Facebook Live Master

Jane M Powers' process for crafting your talk, overcoming objections, and closing sales is nothing short of brilliant! Don't miss crafting your INTROmercial™ in Part 3 of *Speak with Confidence. Sell with Authority* to set you apart from anyone else in your marketplace. That alone is worth thousands of dollars in new clients!

—Tammy Lane, The 7-Figure Business Accelerator, Author of
Facebook Faucet: Turn Up Your Client Flow With Easy Facebook Ads

I'm a speaker, radio show host, bestselling author, coach, and a sales trainer. No matter who you are or what you've done, you need to invest in yourself. When I met Jane M Powers, she listened, asked me questions, and heard me. Together, we developed a talk that delivered my message in my voice, got major results, and never felt "salesy." Then I turned that signature talk into a webinar and a telesummit.

—Judy Hoberman, Selling in A Skirt

Jane M Powers is a world class dynamo who mesmerizes, excites, and inspires. She rides her charisma and boundless energy to move you through your biggest blocks, fears, and obstacles so fast that you're beyond them even before you know what happened. Jane has triumphed over stunning obstacles in her own life. If you're finally ready to leap past what's keeping you from your dreams, she's your solution.

—Rob Schultz, Profit Seduction

NO LONGER PROPERTY OF
ANYTHINK LIBRARIES/
RANGEVIEW LIBRARY DISTRICT

SPEAK

WITH CONFIDENCE

SELL

WITH AUTHORITY

JANE M POWERS

PEACOCK PROUD
P · R · E · S · S

PHOENIX, ARIZONA

NO LONGER PROPERTY OF
ANYTHINK LIBRARIES/
RANGEVIEW LIBRARY DISTRICT

Speak with Confidence. Sell with Authority

Copyright © 2018 by Jane M Powers

First Published in the USA in 2018 by Peacock Proud Press, Phoenix, Arizona
ISBN 978-0-9993675-0-6 paperback
ISBN 978-0-9993675-1-3 eBook

Library of Congress Control Number: 2018942277

All rights reserved. No part of this publication may be reproduced, stored in or introduced into a retrieval system, or transmitted, in any form, or by any means (electronic, mechanical, photocopying, recording or otherwise) without the prior written permission of the publisher. This book is sold subject to the condition that it shall not, by way of trade or otherwise, be lent, resold, hired out, or otherwise circulated without the publisher's prior consent in any form of binding or cover other than that in which it is published and without a similar condition, including this condition being imposed on the subsequent purchaser.

Editors:
Laura L. Bush, PhD, PeacockProud.com
Nina Durfee, NinaDurfee.com
Wendy Ledger, VoType.com

Cover and Interior Layout:
Melinda Tipton Martin, MartinPublishingServices.com

Portrait Photographer:
Stacie Quader, Sassy Stiletto Photography

DISCLAIMER:
This is a work of nonfiction. The information is of a general nature to help readers know and understand more about speaking and selling. Readers of this publication agree that Jane M Powers will not be held responsible or liable for damages that may be alleged or resulting directly or indirectly from their use of this publication. All external links are provided as a resource only and are not guaranteed to remain active for any length of time. Jane M Powers cannot be held accountable for the information provided by, or actions resulting from accessing these resources.

It is with great gratitude and love that I dedicate this book to Glenna Salsbury for her caring mentorship, speaker coaching, and spiritual leadership. Glenna's undying support and belief in me has changed my life.

CONTENTS

FOREWORD

The book you hold in your hands, *Speak with Confidence. Sell with Authority* by Jane M Powers, contains some of the most powerful tools, strategies, and formulas to transform not only your life, but your business. By reading Jane's book, you will experience and discover a new way of doing business that allows you to connect with who you are and why you do what you do. I've been profoundly impressed and inspired by the depth of each and every strategy Jane shares.

This is no ordinary book of hype and suggestions you can't implement. She guides you step-by-step through the process of speaking with confidence and selling with authority. No fluff, no hype—just direct *how to's* and shortcuts to your success. It is a book that allows you to discover and understand the process of going from merely surviving to thriving in business. If you are reading *Speak with Confidence. Sell with Authority*, then I'm guessing you have a desire to do just that. As I always say, "Money's not everything . . . but it's right up there with oxygen."

As a coach, Jane M Powers takes the power of your voice and turns it into a message that sells with meaning and purpose to change lives. Her book not only sheds light on the reality of your brilliance, it also helps you create a talk that commands your message so that the moment you open your mouth, you make money.

I have experienced Jane M Powers speak in person. Although I'm a highly successful speaker myself, Jane knows I never want to follow her on stage. She has no idea just how powerful and good she truly is. Her mind and heart are authentic to her core. I have been speaking for longer than I like to admit, and I agree with Jane that there is no better way to change lives than through the power of one's voice. No matter what life has thrown your way, you must be authentic in your messaging. Jane knows how to help you find your voice, so you find your power. The freedom you experience when you discover your own internal power leads you to the confidence to command your speaking career and authentically sell from any platform.

If you know Jane, then you know she loves getting down to business and getting it done right. She has created two multi-million dollar businesses and knows how to lead people to success. By working with entrepreneurs, Jane has demonstrated time and time again that she is a master at messaging and sales. She is also incredibly successful and enjoys nothing more than seeing her clients grow their business. She loves their success. The methods Jane provides in this book have been proven over and over again by her clients who have successfully grown their businesses.

Speak with Confidence. Sell with Authority offers strategies, formulas, and tips that will give you everything you need to hit the platform and grow as an entrepreneur and a speaking professional. If that isn't enough, Jane delivers endless sales techniques and scripts to help you overcome any sales objection.

I don't know about you, but when someone gives you the cow, why buy the milk? This is one the most profound speaking and sales books on the market. I can attest to Jane's philosophy that there is no way to "play small" or dim your light when you are standing in your truth and expressing it.

I believe Jane M Powers is one of the most powerful women standing strong as she speaks with confidence and sells with authority. She has provided you with an excellent resource to navigate the world of business. In this powerful book, you will discover how to speak up, stand up, and play full out using the power of your voice. Be prepared to transform how you see yourself in the world and how to make a difference while you also make more money.

—Rita Davenport,
Internationally Recognized Hall of Fame Keynote Speaker
and Multimillion Dollar Entrepreneur

ACKNOWLEDGMENTS

I am grateful for the constant love and support of my sister Mary Reese, who has encouraged me to do whatever I desire. She has believed in me and loved me no matter what. She is my rock, my constant support, and my best friend.

There have been many wonderful people along the journey to *Speak with Confidence. Sell with Authority.* My heartfelt appreciation to all the audiences and hosts that have given me the opportunity to enrich their lives.

The people that made this book possible and kept me on track to create it for you: Laura Bush, PhD, Denise Romano, Nina Durfee, Becky Norwood, Melinda Tipton Martin.

INTRODUCTION

The fastest way to gain visibility, grow your list, build your bank account, and make a difference is by speaking, speaking, and more speaking. To gain credibility and establish your presence as an authority in the market, get yourself in front of other people. You cannot afford to be the world's best-kept secret. You have a message to share and a gift for people who can benefit from your genius. In this book, I'm excited to share all I know about speaking, getting booked, and selling your products and services to close the deal. The good news is I'm going to share with you the many places to speak and my fail-proof ways to get booked. Finally, to be a successful entrepreneur, you've got to be great at selling and closing. More good news! If selling and closing make you uncomfortable, know that it's a skill you can learn. I'm about to share some of the best methods to close the deal.

By the way, I never wanted to be in sales or, for crying out loud, to be an entrepreneur. I believed the risk was far too great. I just wanted someone to hand me a paycheck so I could go have fun. I hated the fact that my job always got in the way of my fun. I loved staying active, playing basketball, biking, running, and taking an occasional mid-day nap. Work cramped my style, so I discovered a method that allowed me to work only a few hours daily and play the rest of the time. I found that I could gain more leads by speaking one to many. This method allowed people to get to know me and my services immediately. The more I implemented my shortcuts and systems, the easier I could convert sales. I was determined to capture the lead and close the deal fast. Those basketball games weren't going to win themselves; I needed to hit the court! So I designed successful speaking and sales formulas, which I will share with you in the following chapters. These formulas were brilliant. They resulted in numerous promotions, contest prizes, and a ton of money—for someone else!

You may have guessed it: I knew I had a gold mine with my new systems, and I decided to use those systems to accomplish growth and success for me, not for someone else. I left my job on a Friday afternoon and embarked on the journey of entrepreneurship. Now, twenty-two years later, I'm sharing with you the journey of my success.

Before jumping into the juicy content ahead, I'd like you to know a bit about what makes me tick. At my core, I have a big heart, and I care deeply for others. I am invested in helping and seeing people come into their own. I will love anyone through the dark night of the soul and celebrate their brightest day. People have described me as a little teddy bear with a big heart. In the same breath, they call me the most direct, straightforward, up-front person you will ever meet. I have a way of kicking my clients in the butt to get them moving while, at the same time, giving them a genuine hug. I share this because, throughout this book, you will read and feel my direct delivery and straightforward opinions. I am direct and straightforward because I care and am invested in your success. My book is my commitment to your business, your life, and your success. I do not take that responsibility lightly. I will give you everything I can and not mince words to waste time or energy. The best way to deal with direct advice from me may be to imagine "xoxoxo" at the end of the sentence, because, I promise, the kisses and hugs are there every step of the way.

Over the years, I've come to live my life according to three key values: speak up, show up, and play full out. In **Part 1: Speak Up**, I explain what it means to speak up and be authentically you in your business and in your life. You will learn how to create your own unique style of speaking and stop copying other people. This requires you to identify your own core values and live life according to your truth. Once you find your truth and step into your genius, you will live life from possibility to predictability and not by the conditions in your life. I will walk you through a number of steps to reveal what gets in the way of your success, and I will show you how to S.T.O.P. those things from sabotaging you. In Speak Up, you will get to the bottom of your money story, so you can create a new, more empowering story to close more deals and make more money.

In **Part 2: Show Up**, you will learn to command your power with a brilliant, big-income, big-impact talk using my Speak to Profit formula. I will walk you through crafting your talk. We will begin with the end in mind and move to the first words you will express from the platform. I'm not kidding—you will get everything you need to go out the next day and speak to profit. I have tapped into my thirty-plus years of speaking and sales to create a results-driven formula for a talk that sells. If you are like me, you will want to skip everything else and go to Part 2. Resist the temptation! Why? Awareness of the *inside you* is critical to the message of your *outside you*. The best talk in the world will produce nothing if the inside you is not in order. Be patient. I write this with a big smile because patience is not in my zone of genius. But discipline is, so follow my lead to get the most value from this book. The order of presentation reflects my priority to intentionally support your best interest.

You will love **Part 3: Play Full Out**! This section of the book introduces my unique Ultimate Impact formula to get you booked. You will create your own INTROmercial™ that is sexy and sells. No one else in the marketplace is doing this, nor can they, I dare to say. I will lay out the steps and give you the support needed to create a show-stopping INTROmercial™ that sells in just 17.5 seconds. If that isn't enough, I will also give you the top method to sell with authority. You will learn how to use my C.O.R.E. Code to Close system to master the art of speaking multiple buying languages throughout the sales conversation. You will identify your C.O.R.E. Code and learn to recognize and identify your prospect's buying code. The sales conversation is far more successful when you speak to the C.O.R.E. Code of your buyer. I will give you the basic structure of a sales conversation, along with scripts to use. Last, but not least, I will walk you through the process of overcoming objections with codified questions and responses.

Prepare to have one or more pack-your-bag moments. My colleague, Jay Fiset, describes this as the moment the light bulb turns on and you got what you came for. I am confident this book is your light-bulb experience. Read with a beginner's mind, a mind that is open to seeing and receiving things as new, even if you think you have tried it all. Refrain from thoughts like, "I tried that; it doesn't work," "I know that already," or "That doesn't work for me." See everything as a new possibility for you and your success. I will be with you every step of the way, lending my knowledge, experience, care, and commitment. I've got your back. Enjoy!

PART 1

SPEAK UP

CHAPTER 1
DON'T BE A COPYCAT

Many people who speak, or who want to speak, think they need to sound like other speakers they see as successful. I think you just need to sound like yourself! In fact, I agree with Oscar Wilde, who is credited with saying, "Be yourself. Everyone else is already taken." I love his advice because I see people being copycats all the time. They're not original in the way they show up in their business or in life.

No matter your industry, you need to model, not mimic, your competition, colleagues, or idols. Let me differentiate the two for you.

Modeling comes under the umbrella of social learning theory. We basically learn by what goes on in the brain (cognitive factors) and by environmental factors. We learn within a social setting, and part of what we learn comes from watching others and imitating their behavior. We look at the things that other people do and determine what works and what doesn't work. Our actions and behaviors will then be similar to those patterns or behaviors we've learned through imitation.

Modeling helps us develop socially desirable behaviors and apply those behaviors in various situations. For example, if you demonstrate a sales script to someone, your delivery method will code that pattern of delivery into his or her brain. In the future, the same pattern of delivery will function as a guide for the person's actions. Our first exposure to modeling occurs with our parents and other family members. The way we learned acceptable behaviors, manners, and other social actions involved teaching, positive reinforcement, and punishment when we misbehaved. Then, in school, we experienced peer pressure that dictated what was cool or not cool. We started to model appropriate and inappropriate behaviors to fit in or stand out, whichever we preferred.

Mimicking is many times mistaken for modeling. We watch a mentor and do exactly what they do in the exact style they do it. Why? Because it seems to be working for them, and we don't know any better way. We memorize or impersonate their body language, tone, speech, sayings, their method of delivery, and more. Don't get me wrong. Mimicking has its place in your business and your life. It's one of the best ways to trick yourself into feeling the confidence you need to get out there and do what you've got to do.

In her June 2012 TED talk at TEDGlobal 2012,[1] social psychologist Amy Cuddy explains how body language shapes who we are. She describes how mimicking certain physicality for only a few minutes can raise testosterone levels and lower cortisol levels. According to Cuddy, mimicking can create feelings of power and risk tolerance. I have often used mimicking to achieve success. During my freshman year of college, for example, I tried out for the women's basketball team at Northern Illinois University. NIU was a Division 1 university, which made it a pretty big deal. We would play at other huge universities and compete in tournaments. I made the team as a walk-on and began my fight for survival. Everyone else, with a few exceptions, was on a full-ride scholarship. They were chosen for their athletic accomplishments, and every single one of them had the confidence of a Division 1 player.

I, on the other hand, had the confidence level of . . . well, if truth be told, I had no confidence. None. I was extremely insecure and lacked any sense of self. As a result, other players ate me alive every time I stepped on the court. They would steal the ball, block my shots, or just run right through me. I was the weakest link, and they all knew it. I went back to my dorm room and cried after every practice. I felt demoralized. I thought about Jill Sawin, our senior star player (5' 3" to my 5' 4-1/2"), who commanded the court. At that moment, I decided if I was going to survive, I would need to play like Jill. More importantly, I would need to take on Jill's attitude. I'd be tough and a bit on the cocky side. At the time, I interpreted Jill's attitude as borderline mean, but what I know now is that she was just overflowing with confidence. I had no frame of reference for that kind of confidence. I thought I always had to be nice and put others first in any relationship. Jill was totally self-assured. She tore up any basketball court she stepped onto.

I wanted that same composure and authority. Using a much nicer approach, I did my best to mimic her. I spent extra hours on the court, practicing every chance I got, so that I could apply my own style of play on the court and, hopefully, gain some confidence by elevating my skills and feeling into how Jill might approach her game. The results were not only apparent, but the university paper deemed me the "off the bench bomber" who could nail three pointers. I have met many Jill Sawins in my life, and I have taken from them the foundation and the secret to overcoming fears, doubts, and lack of confidence.

At the age of nineteen, I was determined never to let anything stop me, at least not permanently. I was ready for my second year at Northern Illinois University, and I could not wait to reclaim my spot as the "off the bench bomber." The team was to begin training at the start of the school year, and to everyone's surprise, a new coach had been hired, Rita Horky. She was 6'2" and 250 pounds of mean. The first day she announced, "Walk-ons are not welcome and will not play on any team of mine." I made it as a walk-on my first year, but with Coach Horky's announcement, I was doomed. I had to make the decision to find a new team and never be a walk-on again.

I became my own agent. I had seen enough movies to help me model the big-time scouts and secure myself a new home team. I had no support from my family or friends—only my sheer determination and my ability to model behavior. I entered tryouts and had six colleges bidding for my talents in basketball. I secured a scholarship and earned a starting lineup position as a point guard at College of St. Francis in Joliet, Illinois.

I tell this story because mimicking is a great way to start and gain momentum while you're establishing who you are and how you're going to present yourself in any situation. Mimicking is the way to trick your subconscious mind to accept something as reality. Jill demonstrated exactly what I wanted to accomplish on the court: confidence, command, and star power. Mimicking Jill gave me the determination to go for what I wanted at the time. Tenaciously, I acted like Jill. I went from being a snack on the court to being a smorgasbord of skills and swagger. I became a star player. In fact, I led the team to multiple playoff championships. Mimicking works!

The key to mimicking, though, is to know when to step into your own authentic power. If you never discover your true self and how to express who you are, you will weaken your power. A great example of that is what I call the "Tony Robbins lookalikes." These people do the Tony clap or use his lines, mannerisms, and expressions. They're simply mimicking to the point of being a copycat. Mimicking is a guide and a jumping off point; it's not step-by-step copycatting. It's more like, "Hey, I like that. I'm going to do that and put my own style in it." I see people who have more subdued, quiet personalities trying to be Tony Robbins, and it comes off as canned and fake.

Copycatting happens in the coaching arena when coaches use the same formula, format, or programs handed down from coach to coach. One person in the business of coaching is a huge success, and each of her protégés does almost exactly what she does in her own programs and formulas. There is nothing unique about their business; they are simply being copycats. Are they successful? Sometimes, sure! But I have also witnessed at least four protégés fall into the trap of copycatting and lose themselves. By their own admission, they were chasing the money and not what they love. One of them gained sixty pounds; another burned out nearly to the point of a nervous breakdown; one got cancer; and one was so unhappy she couldn't stand the never-ending pressure to make money or the pace by which she had to do it, so she quit.

Living your truth is about redefining who you are in the work you do. You achieve that when your participation in who you are is high and you have low attachment to who you want other people to be. Minimize your attachment to the outcome. Most of the time we're so stuck on *what's in it for me* that we forget to align with our true values and who we are. We get so wrapped up in generating results that we lose what matters most to us and what's at the heart of what we want to do.

In the absence of our own authentic journey, we run the risk of ending up so far from our goals and desires that it takes hitting a wall to create change. That wall can manifest as cancer, a nervous breakdown, getting fat, or just being so damn miserable you can't stand yourself anymore. It's easy to fall into the trap of doing what everyone else does. When we observe their success, why not copy? I get it! The problem is you cannot create someone else's dream business or life. You must create your own according to your truth.

BE AUTHENTICALLY YOU

The greatest accomplishment in your life is to be YOU! [2] Ralph Waldo Emerson said, "To be yourself in a world that is constantly trying to make you something else is the greatest accomplishment." It's one thing to pattern yourself after something you love about another person: the Dalai Lama's peaceful stance in the world, for example, or Einstein's determination, or Jordan's drive to be the greatest. But it is something else entirely to try to become that person, which is the problem with mimicking when it turns to copycatting. Being a copycat occurs when, instead of patterning yourself after an admirable aspect of a person, you choose to imitate the whole person. Too many people become copycats and lose themselves in the mimicking process, because it's easier to do what others do. To be self-aware and know who you are requires a lot of effort. Why not simply do what others do and create the same success they have in their work? Well, you are not that other person. The unique work you do, only you can do.

Your business must align with your values, goals, and ultimate desires. Anything less will create a problem for you in the long run. You must love what you deliver, and more importantly, it must scream YOU!

I have been coached by some of the greats in the industry. My coaches were accustomed to working with people who wanted to make millions. Money was their sole focus. Therefore, they assumed that I also wanted to make millions, and they coached me the same way. They set up every call for how to make the next five figures or how to "jump the needle" in my business. I got easily swept up in that model and mimicked their actions and strategies. The biggest problem with that was I wanted first and foremost a life of peace and love. For me, money would just be the byproduct of an abundant lifestyle. Using their tools, I drove myself to get greater results, only to find that I felt miserable. The way I was being coached to do business did not align with my core values and goals. I was copying others in the industry and hating what they said I had to do to achieve success.

My success, according to what they said, depended upon industry must-dos. Those must-dos didn't fit my style, my personality, or who I am. Everyone said I should do a launch. The only way I would be successful would be to have a list of thousands upon thousands of email addresses. I also needed the right website and to be on social media. In reality, what I needed was my style of connecting with people and to lead authentically.

In my first year in business, with fewer than three hundred subscribers on my list and employing only a handshake, a smile, and a talk, I created a six-figure income. I don't even think I had a business card. I've been a multiple six-figure coach since then. And it wasn't until the summer of 2016, after five years in the industry, that I finally got a website and a "real" brand. Success is based on what aligns with who you are and what you love. When you force yourself to do it someone else's way, or when you become a copycat because you're being paid thousands and thousands of dollars, you lose yourself. Eventually, you'll also lose clients, income, and your happiness.

Everyone in every industry copies others. Without knowing it, we mimic or copy people we admire, compete with, or strive to surpass. I confess that I, too, was a copycat when I began my own coaching business. I had been speaking since 1986. My first speaking engagement in my early twenties was to a group of juvenile delinquents at a weekend retreat. The experience was, as they say, my baptism by fire. I had never spoken before, except in school, and I had never felt confident delivering any message to more than one person. That presentation started my career in professional speaking. The Lisle Township Youth Committee had scheduled me to present to an audience of more than two hundred juvenile delinquents about leadership, dating, and date rape, a new and evolving topic at the time.

I knew date rape would be a tough subject to present, especially to so many resistant adolescents. But I was fast on my feet. I walked on stage, stood dead center, and belted out a loud belly yell: "AAAAAAHHHHHHHHH!" I had taught this same safety yell to kids to protect themselves from "stranger danger." Yelling on stage, I shocked myself and wowed the crowd, capturing and engaging seemingly resistant juvenile delinquents in seven seconds flat. From that day forward, no one could keep me off the stage. I began speaking in the public and private sectors. At first, I spoke about empowerment, leadership, sexual harassment, and abuse prevention. Then I progressed to speak about sales, leadership, speaking, and business, establishing myself as a darn good speaker who felt confident about my sales, speaking, and business training presentations.

So, why would I call myself a copycat? Not because of the speaking aspect of my business, but because of the coaching business that I built around my speaking. Often when people start something new or venture into the unknown, they experience a lack of confidence. I had a couple of things working against me. First, I was insecure as a coach, and second, I hated the unknown. When I started my spiritual and life coaching business, what compelled me to copycat another person's coaching style was my inability to believe I could use my unique style of speaking in the coaching arena. I studied under great coaches such as Mary Morrissey, Bob Proctor, Gay Hendricks, and others. Mary Morrissey, my dear friend and mentor since 1999, is known for her work as a Visionary and Transformational Spiritual Leader. She is an international speaker, bestselling author, CEO consultant, visionary, and empowerment specialist.

Mary Morrissey has been in the business of transformation for over four decades. In my opinion, she is one of the elite teachers in personal development. I had the privilege of working with her for seven years, coaching and traveling on spiritual pilgrimages, as well as simply enjoying dancing, laughing, crying, and expanding. One of the coolest things Mary did was to speak three times at the United Nations. She also facilitated three different weeklong meetings with His Holiness, The Dalai Lama, and she met with Nelson Mandela in Cape Town, South Africa, to address the most significant issues our world faces. Pretty cool. Under Mary's mentorship, I learned about transcendentalism and the power of creating thought through the teachings of Henry David Thoreau, Ralph Waldo Emerson, Wallace Wattles, and Napoleon Hill. These transcendental authors presented a new way of expressing these concepts for me, so I lost confidence in my own unique expression. Their scholarly writings and teachings sounded very formal and literate. I, on the other hand, used a conversational, direct, down-to-earth speaking style.

Speaking was the focus of my business growth and lead generation. I gave presentations and talks using the *exact* same delivery methods as Mary Morrissey and other transcendentalists. I said things like, "There is a green growing edge of your becoming seeking to emerge through you, by you, as you." Or I would say, "Just as a blade of grass will push through a crack in the cement, growing toward the light, we, too, are being pulled toward a fuller expression of ourselves." Now, don't get me wrong. These are brilliant and profound statements. But I don't naturally speak that way.

To deliver your message, you must be yourself. To be yourself, you have to know who you are: what you want, what you stand for, and what you believe. Without knowing these things, you end up looking and acting like the rest of the world—just like I did when I first began coaching. The single most common reason people copycat others is a lack of confidence in who they are and what they stand for. So, the copycat tendency can be a phase on the way to developing one's own individuality or unique identity in business, career, and life. The problem is, if it lasts too long, it can also be a sign that a person is missing a sense of who she is, and she continues to do business, acting like someone else in order to feel less vulnerable and insecure.

I see this not only in the world of entrepreneurs, but also in business in general. In my niche (speaking and sales strategies), it shows up in startups as well as seven- and eight-figure businesses. Extreme copying is an indicator of low self-esteem or no self-esteem, and/or it indicates an inferiority complex. Copycatting is a survival technique to compensate for feeling that you aren't enough, you're not worthy, or you can't even do it. Copying allows you to temporarily borrow for yourself the self-esteem you imagine this other person has. The real problem is that the amount of success you have is based on who you are and how you express yourself fully. It always comes back to you. You will never outperform your own self-image. If you try to be someone else, you cannot build a business based on your own values and truth. You are a copycat.

When I was impersonating Mary Morrissey, I thought there wasn't a problem using her delivery and presentation style, until I found I was not authentically connecting with my ideal audience. I was connecting with *her* ideal audience and creating a business based on what I thought I should be, not on who I was. I was selling Mary Morrissey's "stuff." It was great "stuff," but it didn't align authentically with me. We set ourselves up for rejection and failure when we try to sell what isn't ours. You can't position the value if you don't feel or experience that it is communicating your unique value. You'll never convince someone else to pay you for that. NO business will survive and thrive if it is created in the image and likeness of someone else.

Your business, talk, presentation, sales style, and manner of expression must be solely built around you, your values, and your truth. I am not saying you won't make money selling someone else's stuff, but most women in my experience define success beyond the ability to make money. I was making the same $150,000 year after year, but I was not thriving in my business. To me, success means thriving in all areas of my life. Being heard and seen for who I am and what I stand for is my definition of success.

CHALLENGE THE IMPOSTER SYNDROME

How do you find true success and feel authentic in your message? You can use teachings, quotes, studies, or concepts from others, but you must bring your own authentic self to life. The best way to stop copying others is to acknowledge there is a little bit (or a lot!) of imposter syndrome going on inside you. Impostor syndrome (also known as impostor phenomenon or fraud syndrome) is a term coined in 1978 by clinical psychologists Dr. Pauline R. Clance and Suzanne A. Imes.[3] It refers to high-achieving individuals marked by an inability to internalize their accomplishments and a persistent fear of being exposed as a fraud. Despite external evidence of their competence, those exhibiting the syndrome remain convinced they are frauds and do not deserve the success they have achieved. Proof of success is dismissed as luck, timing, or because of deceiving others into thinking they are more intelligent and competent than they believe themselves to be.

In their 1978 study, Dr. Clance and Ms. Imes found that many high-achieving women commonly suffer from the impostor syndrome. The syndrome is experienced internally as chronic self-doubt and feelings of intellectual fraudulence. If you experience imposter syndrome, you're in very good company: Denzel Washington, Tina Fey, Kate Winslet, Jodi Foster, and Meryl Streep have each questioned their own success. Even the legendary novelist, poet, and inspirational role model Maya Angelou once said, "I have written eleven books, but each time I think, 'Uh oh, they're going to find out now. I've run a game on everybody and they're going to find me out.'"[4]

Impostor feelings can be divided into three subcategories: (1) feeling like a fake, (2) attributing success to luck, and (3) discounting success. Let's look at each of these three subcategories.

1) FEELING LIKE A FAKE

You believe you don't deserve your success or professional position. You feel as if somehow, you've tricked or deceived others. This is the undying thought and fear of being "found out" or discovered. People who feel this way identify with statements such as, "I haven't done what I'm teaching others to do, and they will find out," or "I'm afraid they'll discover how much I don't know."

I experienced these thoughts and feelings many times when I started my coaching business in 2010. I felt this way every time I tried something new. I didn't feel confident in my ability to pull it off. For example, when I began teaching people how to sell from the stage, whether asking for money or making a free offer, I felt like a fake or a fraud. I believed I was not qualified to teach this because I had not sold from the stage as much as others had. I believed that if I didn't close over $500,000 from the stage, I didn't know what I was doing. In addition, I was convinced I would be found out. I even believed that the people who were selling over $500,000 from stage would call me out and expose me. Since I grew up thinking I was the dumb kid, I clearly thought there was no place at the top for me.

The imposter syndrome plagues us all. We're in a never-ending battle to disarm our doubts and fears. What is it, specifically, that you are afraid people will find out about you? Pin down your specific doubts about yourself. Write your doubts and fears here:

I am afraid

_____

_____

_____

I am afraid

_____

_____

_____

I doubt that I can

_____

_____

_____

Other thoughts you repeatedly say to yourself

_____

_____

_____

Many of my clients and colleagues find that thought patterns prevent them from moving forward and doing new things. Plagued by their own self-sabotaging thoughts, they tend not to sell as well, and their results suffer. Again, I want to emphasize the amount of money you are making, how many clients you have, or the outside results you achieve are not what it's all about. It's about the confident feeling you experience as you navigate your success.

2) ATTRIBUTING YOUR SUCCESS TO LUCK

You're convinced that your success is due to external reasons and not to your own internal abilities. People with these feelings fear they will not be able to succeed the next time. They say of their success or achievements, "I just got lucky this time," or "It was beginners luck," or "It was a fluke." Attributing my success only to luck was one of my most persistent imposter syndrome afflictions. Ironically, I NEVER believed I was lucky or blessed. My greatest fear? Not being able to sustain or duplicate the success I achieved.

In 2003, I decided to get my real estate license, despite my belief I was the worst test taker ever and that I wasn't a smart kid. I made my way through high school by cheating off my smart friend, Dana Work, so there was no way I could pass a state real estate exam. I enrolled in every real estate class and studied endless hours as I continued to struggle with my story, "I am going to fail." Despite this fear-based thinking, I kept moving forward. I scheduled my test date, walked in, sat down, and watched as the test administrator began the ninety-minute timer. Everyone in the room immediately started calculating how many square feet were in an acre, defining what an agency is, and answering a number of other questions I had never seen in my life. I was sweating like a mad woman. My heart raced, and I swore I wasn't going to make it. I completed the test and checked my work in just twenty minutes. "OH NO!" I thought. "No one else is done. What did I miss?"

I walked out and sat in the waiting area, expecting to hear the news that I had failed. Instead, the instructor called my name, handed me a paper, and said, "Thanks." Disappointed, I asked her when I could retake the test. She looked up at me and asked, "Why? You passed! And pretty quickly, I might add."

I wish I could say this was the last time I doubted myself, but it wasn't—and it won't be. For years, I have held live, three-day events and attributed my mid-six-figure results to beginner's luck. In reality, I have worked hard to make these events successful, meaning they are valuable for the entrepreneurs who attend and financially successful for me. You, too, may find that the imposter syndrome creeps up on you. The trick is to be aware and notice the story you make up about yourself. Because of the difficult things that happened to me growing up, I told myself that I would always be living a *less-than* life.

The best way to overcome your disempowering story is to tell a better version of it. For example, BECAUSE of what happened to me, there is no one better than I to do the work I do. I often frame a better version of my story as a question. BECAUSE of my *less-than life* thinking, who better to help others out of that thinking than me? Rather than feed your negative stories or thoughts, transform them into empowering stories or thoughts. How? We'll dive more deeply into that later.

3) DISCOUNTING YOUR SUCCESS

Entrepreneurs tend to downplay or discount their success. They say, "It's not a big deal," "It's not that important," "I'm not as good as my competitors," or "I did well because I'm offering a lower price point." If this sounds like you, then another thing to look at is how well you accept compliments. The two go hand in hand.

I discounted my own success by constantly comparing myself to others. "Comparanoia" (a term coined by my dear friend, Lois Blumentha) is a bad habit to break. The killer of all successes and dreams is comparing yourself to others. You are NOT someone else. You are living a purpose different from every other person on the planet. I believe we are all here to do what is ours to do, but we tend to look at what others are doing and want to do the same. Comparanoia traps us into another way of being a copycat. You will never live up to someone else's purpose or mission. You can only live up to your own. Comparing yourself to others is destructive, but even worse is comparing where you are to your vision of where you want to be. You will always fall short of your vision when you measure your results today.

Allow me to break that down for you: if you want to be a world-class speaker but have never hit a stage, your results will disappoint you. If your vision is to be a seven-figure earning entrepreneur and you haven't made more than a buck fifty, you'll be disappointed each time you measure where you are compared to where you want to be. Instead, keep your eye focused on your vision and goals to see that everything you do is the building block or stepping stone to that result. "All things necessary," says Genevieve Behrend in her book, *Your Invisible Power*. [5] Everything you do is necessary to get you to your vision. Your vision is constantly expanding; therefore, you will always fall short. In other words, stop comparing your beginning to someone else's middle, and start appreciating everything and everyone. Use the people in your industry as examples of your future success. They are living proof that you can be successful in your work. I look at Brendon Burchard, Lisa Sasevich, and Mary Morrissey as living proof that I, too, can create whatever I desire in my work. You can do it, too!

Stop being a copycat or mimicking others by giving your feelings and thoughts a voice. Start by acknowledging your feelings of fear, doubt, or competition. Admit that you suffer from comparanoia. Be aware when you engage in comparing thoughts and feelings. Awareness is the first step to change. You may not catch yourself in comparanoia if you don't pay attention to your automatic thoughts and patterns.

Next, set up a system of structure and support so you can discuss those feelings with others. Doing this helps you understand you're not alone. This support helps you relate differently to the thoughts in your head, which aren't actually your thoughts anyway. They're just the common brain patterns of human beings. I refer to these brain patterns as "automatic thoughts." Automatic thoughts are the underlying, unquestioned thoughts that affect how you perceive an event or situation. These thoughts are so automatic that they happen very fast. You may not even notice them, but they affect your perception of your circumstances, your results, and what's possible for you in the future.

Here is a bit about the brain and how these automatic thoughts become a part of our everyday lives. When we initially learn something, the pathway or connection is weak and needs to be developed. The more frequently we think a particular thought, the stronger the pathway becomes, forming an automatic habit of thinking. Essentially, we are training our brain to a new thought or pattern. Consider learning to ride a bike. At first your primary focus is to stay balanced, eyes forward, grip the handlebars, and steer in your desired direction. The more you practice, the stronger your bike-riding patterns become.

Eventually, rewiring your thought patterns is just like riding a bike (sorry, I couldn't resist). You begin operating with automatic thoughts or patterns. A strong brain pathway has been created and a new system is operating in your mind. You don't have to think about it or focus on the basics. These new thoughts have become patterns in your mind.

Whether you are riding a bike or starting a new business, your brain must create patterns and pathways to enable you to fully operate at your best. You have a few hurdles to jump as you develop new patterns—the old patterns! Just like riding a bike, your brain works the same way in forming how you think about yourself, determining the level of confidence you have in yourself in a particular area of your life. As a child, your thoughts about yourself form from the messages you hear and believe from people who are important and influential for you. For example, my sister continually teased me when I was growing up. She called me "fat, dumb, and stupid." For years, I would hide from her when I was eating. I was afraid she would tease me more.

Many kids are bullied and teased at school. Because I was teased as a child, I was plagued even as an adult. These thoughts automatically surfaced when I tried on clothes, ate certain foods, or had what felt like a "fat" day. Okay, the worst was when I would go into a dressing room. What do they do with the lights in there, anyway? Imperfections that I never even knew existed would light up. The imperfections probably weren't real, but my pattern of fat thinking was so ingrained that I would think, "I'm fat," "I look terrible in this outfit; it shows every bulge," "Don't eat that; you'll get fat," or "I'm disgusting."

The ironic part of my belief is that I was lucky if I cleared four feet in height and fifty pounds soaking wet. The repetition of the information I kept rehearsing created an automatic thought pattern. These and many other automatic thoughts are habits. They are the thoughts that trigger, consciously or unconsciously, negative feelings and reactions to the circumstances of life. The good news is we can S.T.O.P. these patterns and change them.

CHAPTER 2
S.T.O.P.

Speaking with confidence and selling with authority requires diligence in managing the old patterns that run through your mind. To move through times when you feel like an imposter and lead your mind to an empowering action, use my S.T.O.P. formula. This step-by-step process begins with your feelings, and I've designed the formula to re-pattern your brain.

Things happen in our lives, some good, some bad. We all have feelings and need to navigate emotions effectively without getting stuck in the feelings too long. Everything we do results in a feeling, and I firmly believe we must experience all of them! Feelings are a natural part of being human. I, myself, am a "feeler," and I want my feelings to be validated fully before I begin to turn them around. What does it mean to have your feelings validated? It means you allow yourself to express them verbally. Whether you verbalize them to a partner, spouse, friend, or therapist doesn't matter. My entire philosophy is based on finding your voice, which includes giving your feelings the freedom to flow.

In my experience, however, people don't always pay attention to their feelings and emotions. They try, instead, to "stuff" their feelings. I believe that feelings and emotions are meant to be felt, expressed, and transformed. If we don't get our feelings out, they go somewhere else, becoming either internal or external spillage. Sigmund Freud is attributed with saying, "Unexpressed emotions will never die. They are buried alive and will come forth later in uglier ways." In other words, unexpressed feelings get stored away in our own system or they spill out onto others at the most inopportune times.

Many people unconsciously stuff their feelings out of habit. For some people, feelings are inconvenient or exhausting. But emotions are a natural response to living. Suppressing or repressing emotions is not. When we do not release our feelings, even healthy emotions become physically and mentally toxic, stealing away our self-confidence, self-esteem, and self-love. Stuffed emotions cause us to act out in undesirable ways that result in addiction, depression, or codependency. Problematic overachieving and underachieving are also symptoms of toxic emotions.

Living in a body where so much emotion has been suppressed can be quite uncomfortable. You can try to fool yourself by thinking you have overcome these memories by ignoring them or pushing them to the side, but they will continue to fester deep within you, gnawing at you from the inside out and leading to any number of symptoms: insomnia, headaches, stomach problems, and fatigue. The adverse effects that stuffed emotions put on your body can cause chronic or deadly illness as well. Stress weakens your immune system, making you prone to devastating illnesses and autoimmune disorders.

Not only will stuffed feelings have an adverse internal effect on your physical system, but they will affect your outside world. Unexpressed feelings and emotions limit you by impeding your relationships, stealing your joy, stealing your vitality, robbing you of inner peace, and disempowering you. Most of the time you don't even know it, but inside you are like a ticking time bomb. One day, your emotions could explode and wreak havoc in your life.

Have you ever overreacted or taken your negative frustrations, feelings, or emotions out on an unsuspecting victim? I think every driver on the road is a likely candidate for me if I have an unexpressed feeling. I am still a masterpiece in progress. I don't exercise much restraint on the road; it's just too easy and deliciously anonymous to be expressive behind the wheel.

There was a time in my life when I was profoundly aware of my unexpressed emotions. That doesn't count my childhood, because, indeed, I could not express an emotion, no matter what. In my teens and early adult years, every time I played any sport, I spilled unexpressed emotions everywhere. I played every sport available to me. I was intense playing basketball, ice hockey, football, softball, or soccer. Because of my childhood and my lack of ability to express my emotions, I was a time bomb.

I am not proud to admit this, but I got into many fights—yes, all-out physical Ultimate Fighting Championship-style fights. I was angry inside, and unfortunately, in the sports I played, there was a ton of physical contact. Something would push my buttons or trigger me, and I would erupt inside, only to find myself going at it with an opponent. At 5' 4-1/2" on a really good day, I didn't have a lot of bulk to my stature, but what I did have was a ton of pent-up anger and emotion. Feelings can be very painful, especially when we have never allowed ourselves to fully experience them. But once we learn to allow our feelings, we discover that it is not our feelings that hurt us. It is denying our feelings that causes us the most pain.

Denied or unexpressed emotions will find an escape hatch, skillfully or unskillfully. We all know when we feel bad and when we feel good. A bad feeling creates a desire to feel better, so we unconsciously start to dump or get the feeling out. If we don't do this in a skillful manner, our feelings dump or spill out onto others. Sports was my emotional outlet.

Here are some ways to recognize if your emotions are begging to be expressed:

- You startle easily.
- Your senses are overly keen.
- Your hearing is extra sensitive.
- Your skin is sensitive.
- You are easily frightened.
- Your taste is acute; foods taste stronger than usual.
- Odors are more pungent; things smell stronger than usual.
- Your nerves are overly reactive.

- You snap or are short with others.
- You are sensitive to light.

We usually refer to these symptoms or conditions as "stress." We blame the world around us for the stressors we face. In my experience, stress is merely unexpressed emotions. What emotions are you not expressing? The first step to excavating buried emotions is awareness. We become aware of our emotions by paying attention to our triggers—our hot buttons or the things that make us strongly react. Those triggers signal where to start digging for our feelings. Once you identify your feelings, allow them to surface. And once they surface, allow yourself to feel them. Experiencing yourself and your feelings in ways that you may be unaccustomed to is not easy, but it's the key to emotional freedom.

Our feelings are the fuel for everything we do. Feelings create our desires and actions. For example, feeling bad triggers a desire or a need to feel good. Therefore, we search for what will help us feel good. I am convinced that the more you feel, the more you live. I experienced a complicated childhood, including my mother's early death, alcoholism in my family, and sexual abuse that resulted in some truly deep, negative emotions. I did not know how to experience my feelings when I was growing up. Once I began expressing them, I had a much greater capacity for positive feelings. The key is not to "get over" your feelings, but to relate to your feelings in a way that transforms you and your life.

I've developed a formula to help me move from my feelings to results. This quick formula allows you to feel the feelings and move on. Do you sometimes feel like Bill Murray's character in *Groundhog Day?*[6] Do you ever set your goals or start your day with the best of intentions, only to encounter familiar roadblocks, obstacles, and negative feelings that stop you? Everyone experiences reoccurring feelings, triggers, or patterns that can block us from experiencing joy, enthusiasm, and intentional actions.

I don't know about you, but I get tired of the same negative patterns or triggers showing up repeatedly in my life. But it isn't the experience of old feelings and patterns that's the problem. It's how we relate to them. What works best is to be aware of the feelings, feel them, give a kind glance to the related patterns, and quickly move on to fulfill our goals and dreams. My friend and mentor, Mary Morrissey, used to say, "Many live ninety years and many live ninety years, one year at a time." That is a very profound concept and TRUE. If we string enough amazing hours together, we get an amazing day. And if we string enough of those amazing days together, we get an amazing week, then year, and then an amazing life!

How do we live an amazing life? Have an amazing business? Amazing everything? By staying fully awake and committed to our relationship with our feelings. Here is a formula I created to help you move from feeling the feelings to setting an intention, so that you can use the feelings to your advantage. It will help you to stop living Groundhog Day over and over again. It's pretty simple. You just have to S.T.O.P.

State your preference.
Trigger Curiosity.
Open to Imagination.
Put it into Action.

Let me break it into more detail for you.

STATE YOUR PREFERENCE

The first step to moving on from your feelings is to decide what you want. If something shows up that you don't like, clarify what you would prefer. For example, if you are afraid to make the sales call for fear of rejection, failure, or maybe you can't express the value you provide, state your preference. "I would rather feel confident and know that the call is really about connecting and creating a relationship, not about closing the deal. And if it is just about relationship and I know I am good at that, then I prefer to feel confident."

TRIGGER CURIOSITY

Ask yourself how it would be to feel confident when you make the call or do the thing that you're putting off. Be curious about *if/then*. In the moment, ask these questions: What if I could? What if it is possible? What if there were a way? Or simply, what if . . . ?

OPEN TO IMAGINATION

When you ask what-if questions, your mind begins to create a picture to fill in the blank, and you open to imagination. The mind sees in pictures. If I say, "Hawaii," for example, your mind may see a beach, crystal clear water, a lounge chair, and a little drink with a little umbrella. If I mention your car, your kitchen, or your child, your mind recalls the visual of that thing or person. Even better, if I tell you NOT to see Lady Liberty standing tall in the harbor, you cannot help but create a visual of the Statue of Liberty. This process of imagining is exactly how you transform a preference into results. You vividly imagine what it would look like to have, be, or do what you prefer.

Imagination is the quickest way to create something, good or bad. In 1989, my speaking coach, Glenna Salsbury, taught me a powerful formula: Vividness x Imagination = reality. I've adapted and enhanced her formula to read: Vividness x Imagination x Emotion = Reality^2. You square the results by adding emotion to the formula. By feeling the results that you want to create, you supercharge the equation. Feelings are related to what you desire, not to what you have not yet created. Let me explain. Many people *want* because they don't *have*, and the mind doesn't understand the difference between "don't want" and "want." The mind only responds to emotion.

VIVIDNESS X IMAGINATION X EMOTION =

$REALITY^2$

For example, if you have no money to pay your bills, your emotions come from a place of not having, unless you intentionally feel from a place of having. Some call this "living as if." You think, talk, feel, and live as if you already have what you prefer. For this to work, you must feel from curiosity and not from what is or isn't. Hint: sometimes when we imagine what we would love or prefer, we begin to think about the *how*. But at this point in the formula, how is none of your business. The most important component of this formula is the gradual move into possibility. If you find yourself going to the *how* (or seeing and obsessing about what is not yet happening), go back to the very beginning and state your preference.

PUT IT INTO ACTION

When you stay curious and imagine the results, you can then put it into action. Doing is the fastest way to move through blocks and old paradigms. Action changes the energy or focus of your mind. A "doing" distraction for even just a moment can re-pattern the mind to allow you to get back on course. Act on the preference and do one thing in the direction of the new thought. When you get off track, S.T.O.P. Then use the power of your mind to bring you back into focus.

It's not always easy to S.T.O.P. You've taken a long time to develop negative thought patterns that keep repeating. Sometimes it seems those thoughts have taken on a life of their own, and they won't go away without a fight. My S.T.O.P. method will help you ease out of old patterns and into new, empowering patterns. Be patient, be persistent, and be successful!

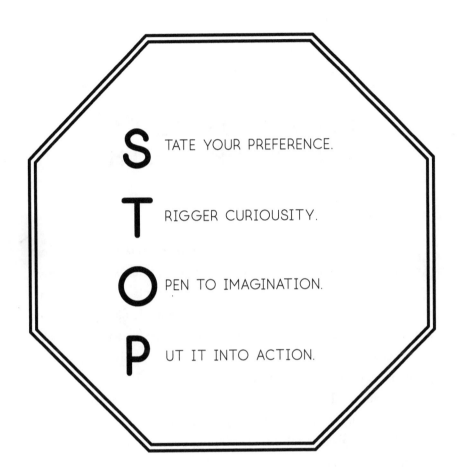

STATE YOUR PREFERENCE.

TRIGGER CURIOUSITY.

OPEN TO IMAGINATION.

PUT IT INTO ACTION.

CHAPTER 3

FIND YOUR VOICE
AND YOUR TRUTH

According to Dictionary.com, the definition of *truth* is different from what is true. *Truth* is defined as: "1. the true or actual state of a matter: *He tried to find out the truth.* 2. conformity with fact or reality; verity: *the truth of a statement.* 3. a verified or indisputable fact, proposition, principle, or the like: *mathematical truths.* 4. the state or character of being true. 5. actuality or actual existence. 6. an obvious or accepted fact; truism; platitude. 7. honesty; integrity; truthfulness."

The definition I want to focus on is "statement or idea that is true or accepted as true." We accept so many things as truth, but are they really true? We each go through life developing our own unique filters and monitoring systems that help us determine what is right or wrong, true or untrue, good or bad. The greatest challenge is to determine what is our truth versus what we were told was true or what we have interpreted in the past as being true. We might believe something is true, but how do we discern if it is our truth? Does the fact that we inherited or learned something from our parents, teachers, family, or anyone else in our lives make it true?

We come into this world with a clean slate, a brand new blank canvas. Before we can even pick up a brush, someone else slaps some paint on our canvas. "Stop crying" is one color slapped on our canvas. As we grow older, we are told not to cross the street, not to talk to strangers, and, "Why can't you be like your brother?" As we develop truths for ourselves, our little minds are flooded with messages—good, bad, or indifferent. We learned to navigate the busy, noisy world by observing, listening, and interpreting external messages. It turns out that these messages and our interpretations of them kept us safe and sane and helped us fit in. The biggest problem with the system, though, is that it buried the truth of who and how we are. We accept as true what we heard and were told.

What is your truth? I believe our truth is buried under all the messages, beliefs, and stories that play in our minds. These are unconscious and automatic patterns of thinking. For example, I grew up the youngest of seven kids. The messages I heard from my family were rarely empowering or uplifting. One message I heard over and over again was, "You are fat, dumb, and stupid." My sister teased and criticized me for many years in this way. As a result, "fat, dumb, and stupid" became a truth for me about myself—not in physical reality, but in my mind. I heard that message enough times that I believed it. As a result, I struggled and lacked confidence in myself for most of my life. Because I believed I was the dumb kid and wouldn't do well no matter what, I did poorly on tests in school. I didn't believe I could do well because that's what I was told. I turned that message into a truth based on repetitive, constant input over the years.

How does this conditioning work? It's actually very simple. Our mind is one of our most powerful tools. Our mind is the vehicle for our awareness of the world and our experiences. It enables us to think and to feel. Our mind is the faculty of our consciousness and thought. As intriguing as it is, I won't go deep into the science of the mind and brain, but I do want to give you the basics and how to apply them easily to your everyday life.

You have a conscious and subconscious mind. The conscious mind is your present-time awareness at. You are aware of what is going on outside as well as mental activity on the inside. You are aware, for example, of the chair you are sitting on, what you see and hear, your breath. The subconscious mind (the automatic mind) consists of information stored from past experiences. The subconscious mind is accessed by a specific trigger that brings memories to your consciousness automatically and without warning.

Think of your mind as a computer. What sits on your desktop is like your conscious mind. What gets stored on your computer (your contacts, calendar, programs, spreadsheets, and more—many of which you don't even pay attention to) is your subconscious mind. The subconscious contains everything that has ever happened to you, and it's being supplied with information from your conscious mind through conditions or surroundings, basically what's happening every second. I refer to the subconscious mind as your switching station. Sometimes I refer to the subconscious mind as the Captain of the Vessel.

To illustrate, this experience might ring a bell for you. You get up in the morning and your spouse, family member, or coworker says to you, "You look a little cranky."

"No, I'm good," you say.

"No, I know that look. It screams cranky."

You continue to defend and deny any evidence of crankiness. The person persists, pointing out, again, that you're cranky. What happens next? You get cranky!

Here's what's happening behind the scenes. Your subconscious mind is unable to distinguish fact from fiction. The subconscious mind gets input from the senses and from the conscious mind. Thoughts run through your mind continuously, good and bad. The subconscious mind receives the input and searches for any evidence from the past, present, and other sources to provide a match to it. As you defend your mood, the subconscious mind is busy providing you with evidence about your bad hair day and the kids being late, things that caused you to be cranky in the past. As a result, you become cranky.

Here's another example. If I say to you, "Lemon, lemon candy, sucking on a lemon," your mouth starts to water. The subconscious mind automatically recalls a time you sucked on a lemon or anything that made you pucker. Our subconscious mind evokes those memories, and we consciously label those thoughts as true. Using my former truth of being fat, dumb, and stupid, let's break this down. I heard the statement repeatedly over the years. My subconscious mind stored the statement with all the other memories or events that supported it. When I was the first one to sit down in the spelling bee, for instance, that event was stored in the "fat, dumb, and stupid" file. The more "fat, dumb, and stupid" moments I had, the more that became my truth.

We set up what we think is our truth through repetition or trauma. It's no different than good ol' Pavlov's dog.[7] Our old beliefs, stories, and patterns are not our truth. But until we feed new information into our subconscious mind, we live according to these old habits of thinking. It is vital that we re-inform our mind of our truth. Henry Ford is attributed with saying, "Whether you think you can or think you can't, you are right." Our habits of thinking start from what we think about and notice. When we notice something, our subconscious mind accesses patterns, stories, and paradigms that are very seductive.

Paradigms are the experiences we make real. They describe the truths we define based on our experiences. In the past, if someone complimented me, my mind would access "fat, dumb, and stupid," so I would draw attention to my love handles. My paradigm, or truth, was that I am fat. We all have experienced failure in life. Our story around those failures is what creates a paradigm. The subconscious mind operates according to old paradigms.

How do you find your truth and move through these patterns and paradigms of believing? You can never outlive or outperform your self-image. What might feel true is not always true. Your perceived truth is the story you tell about who you are. It is *not* always who you really are. It is based on your story. Your ability to allow greater good or success is based on your ability to transform your story, and thus transform your self-image.

Think of self-image as a high bar in your mind. You measure everything according to the bar, including your big ideas and dreams. You likely unconsciously reject anything above the bar, things you think you cannot attain or don't deserve. To make a change, stretch and massage your subconscious mind slowly. For example, if you believe you are terrible at sales, don't go out and make fifty sales calls all at once. That only reinforces your subconscious belief. To achieve success, your belief must align with your desired outcome. You can't think success and failure at the same time. They are two opposing thoughts, and the mind doesn't have the ability to rationalize or think through your intention. The subconscious mind will bring about the result you believe to be true. In other words, the subconscious mind is a magnet to your dominant belief.

Instead, get at the mindset just above what you think you can do. Before making sales calls or taking action, set an intention that you believe you can achieve. Maybe you make one outbound call and decide you will connect with one person easily. Suspend the need to sell. Simply connect. I call this softening of expectations "massaging" the subconscious mind.

The work is to massage the subconscious mind and turn your limiting stories or paradigms into a desired outcome. This is simple and straightforward, but it's not always easy. I have experienced this work firsthand. For years, I believed I was the *kid who*. You name it; I believed it. If we are told something enough times, it becomes our story or our truth, and I was told repeatedly that I was too stupid to amount to anything. I experienced more than my fair share of both verbal and physical trauma in my family, which resulted in many inaccurate beliefs or paradigms. You may have experienced unfavorable conditions that set you up to believe things that just aren't true. Good news! Anyone can transform beliefs into powerful, positive results.

How can you go from an inherited or ingrained belief about yourself to knowing what is really true? By following three easy steps: (1) Realize the story. (2) Release and re-pattern the story. (3) Align the story. Let me explain.

REALIZE THE STORY YOU BELIEVE IS TRUE ABOUT YOURSELF

The first step is to find what is true about you despite what others have said or done. When you realize the story you tell about yourself, you can transform everything in your life. In the past, I told myself that I was not smart enough. I grew up hearing that I was fat, dumb, and stupid. My father discouraged me from law school because, in his opinion, I was too dumb. Another story I told for years and years was that God forgot me. I concluded very early in life that God forgot me because no God would allow this form of abuse to happen to anyone. That story resulted in my feeling abandoned and alone. It was a painful story to carry, even paralyzing at times. I needed to put this belief into perspective, or I would never find fulfillment or success.

What is your *God forgot me* story? Make a list of the statements or stories you tell about yourself. Do you say you are fat? Do you believe you are never going to amount to anything? What excuses do you make? My favorite excuse to myself and others was, "If you grew up in a family like mine, you, too, would be behind in your success." That terrible story felt true to me. We all have stories about ourselves, good or bad. Identify your stories and statements. Examples of crippling beliefs: "I'm not smart enough," "I have no degree," "I'm not good at speaking," "I am terrible at sales," or "I'm too [old, young, tall, skinny, fat]!"

People also make very definitive statements about their current life or business conditions. Conditions happen based on our beliefs. Remember, the subconscious mind is a magnet to your dominant belief or the strongest story you tell. If you believe you can't get the promotion because you are too old, you won't get the promotion. If you want to lose that last five pounds but you believe you can't lose weight no matter what, guess what? Those darn five pounds will not go away. Trust me, I know! Realize your story by listening to your language and your thoughts. Make a list, keep it handy, and continue to add to it. More stories will bubble up as you continue to experience more growth and success.

RELEASE AND RE-PATTERN THE STORY

The second step is to release and re-pattern the old stories and habits so that you can determine what is true. If a story or statement that you think or tell about yourself is not positive or empowering, you will do well to release it. The goal is to own the real truth about you and to understand that others were wrong. You are not what someone else has said about you. You are not what happened to you. Stories that you have been telling yourself and believing for years feel real. I swore God did forget me. It felt so real, and I could show evidence of it when things did not work out for me. It became a fact. Transforming what feels like a fact into a new truth requires thinking differently and releasing the old story.

Our truth or new story is superior to the facts we believed or even the facts that we see every day. Facts can change; truth is constant. When we shift our thought, we create a new truth. Using your list from Step 1 (Realize the Story), design a new truth. Next to each story or belief, write a more empowering statement. For example, if one of your stories is that you are too old, next to it write why your age is a benefit to the world. In your new story, emphasize your variety of experiences or your accumulation of knowledge to share. My more empowering story about being too dumb was the truth that I graduated from college with a 4.0 grade point average. How does someone too dumb do that? What is your more empowering story that allows you to release and ultimately re-pattern your thinking?

Re-patterning takes discipline and attention. Re-patterning happens when you reduce the power of the old, negative story and increase the impact of the new, more empowering story. I live in Phoenix, Arizona, where temperatures climb to 115 degrees or more. When I get into my car during the summer months, I don't grab handfuls of heat and throw it out the window. I turn the air conditioner on high and wait for the cool air to take over the blistering heat. This is a form of re-patterning. Your radio is another example. You have the control to turn up the volume or turn it down. The same is true with your thinking and storytelling. You can't just toss out the old story. You have to shift focus to the new.

A great trick to help you transform your truth is to practice being *grateful in all*. No matter the conditions, be grateful. Many of my clients, both entrepreneurs and corporations, find it challenging to be *grateful in all*. My clients are very happy when they enroll a client or close a deal. They see money coming in, and they are grateful for the *results*. Let's flip the story and understand the difference. A client connects but doesn't convert, doesn't enroll, and bombs. She is not grateful for this *situation*. She may be frustrated, mad, or want to throw in the towel. I've been there myself. Being grateful for *something* is easy when things work out the way you planned. When they don't work out, it's time to practice being *grateful in all*. Some call this finding the silver lining. *Grateful in all* is turning up the volume on the good, no matter how little good there appears to be. Gratitude for everything is the quickest way to change your thinking.

Every time you are *grateful in all*, you develop your capacity to re-pattern and write a new story. Gratitude bypasses the stories and beliefs that keep us from covering up our truth. When you open up to knowing that truth is beyond the facts, you are empowered to make a conscious choice instead of a reactive choice.

ALIGN THE STORY

The third step to defining your truth is to align your new story. Transformation requires thinking in alignment with the business and life you want to create. Three ways of thinking that will put you in alignment with your success: (a) be conscious of abundance; (b) expand your awareness of what is possible; (c) form an image.

Transformation into your truth first requires creating **a consciousness of abundance**. Since 2004 I have been mentoring a young man who was raised in less than ideal conditions. His family continuously struggled for more. Just when they would get past disaster, something else would happen, and they would lose it all again. They never made it beyond the struggle. While most of us are not living those dramatic physical conditions, we are often there mentally and emotionally.

Sometimes feeling good or acknowledging improvement or success seems too good to be true. We hit the glass ceiling—an unacknowledged barrier to success. Gay Hendricks says it best in his book, *The Big Leap: Conquer Your Hidden Fear and Take Life to the Next Level.*[8] He describes the "upper limit problem," something virtually all of us face. In brief, parts of us are programmed to stay safe, to not shine or stand out from the crowd. As a result, we each create our own internal glass ceiling. We limit our success, wealth, health, and happiness for fear of the consequences. We are held back because of a set of core beliefs that we will fail, we will be alone, or we are not enough.

This doesn't have to be the case. You can align with a more empowering story or thought. You can create a new upper limit. Alignment with a new story diminishes the power of the old fears and shifts the focus of your creativity and drive to what is your unique gift. Aligning with your new story or new upper limit opens you to greater possibilities and thoughts of more abundance.

I have studied the conscious and subconscious mind for over twenty-five years, and I am very familiar with the Law of Consciousness. If you have a consciousness of abundance, it brings more and more good to you. If you don't have a consciousness of abundance, you experience lack. Or you may attract money or good, but no matter what you do, it doesn't stick around. Even worse, you don't attract anything at all. You may attribute your fluctuation in success or finances to bad luck or believe that's just how it goes for you. You might have a mentality that the other shoe is about to drop. Inevitably, the other shoe does drop. That's how the Law of Consciousness works. That kind of thinking is just a bad habit. It is the story you tell. Tell a more empowering story of abundance and invoke the Law of Consciousness by purposely thinking thoughts of wealth and prosperity.

The second way of thinking to transform your truth and align with your new story is to **expand your awareness of what is possible**. Nelson Mandela said, "It always seems impossible until it's done." [9] The old self settles into the status quo. You may believe it is what it is. Instead, ask, "What if . . . ?" You challenge the old thinking by triggering curiosity. Think of a time that you were curious about something, anything. Curiosity triggers the imagination, and you become aware of more possibilities. *What if* is frustrating to the status quo of the mind. Ask yourself right now, "What if . . . ?" and fill in the blank. What if an event host called you out of the blue? What if you find the love of your life? What if you create a six-figure business this year? *What if?* When I ask, "What if . . . ?" it puts an immediate stop to my doubtful thinking and opens me to what is possible. Anything is possible. Are you willing to accept that as your new truth? Seeing what is possible inspires new ideas, images, resources, and a flow of understanding that opens us up to choices and decisions we can put into action.

The third way of thinking to transform into your truth requires **forming an image**. Make it concrete by creating a vision board, a collage of pictures that represent your greatest desires. Plant an image or picture in your mind of how you want your life to look. I had a friend who created a vision board of her future slender self. She loved the look of the slender woman she posted on her board. She looked at it every day and fell in love with the image. She wasn't fond of the hairstyle, but all else was perfect. To her surprise, at the conclusion of her latest hair appointment, she walked out with the exact hairstyle on the vision board. She wasn't thrilled, but she had to laugh at the power of the image in her mind. She loved that image into reality.

You, too, can love an image into reality. You can create an image to grow your business or lose a few pounds. The image is up to you. I suggest you create an image for every aspect of your life. An image triggers the imagination, which then activates the subconscious mind. This is very important! The subconscious mind does not distinguish between fact or fiction. It has one job, and one job only, and that is to do exactly what you command it to do. The simple gesture of forming an image is a command. Remember when I gave you the suggestion of lemon and it made your mouth water? The subconscious mind is a repository of everything you have experienced and done, and it will elicit a response, emotionally and physically. You can trigger the same kind of concrete response from whatever vision you focus on.

If you want to grow your business, speak on the big stage to a thousand people, or lose those darn five pounds, you must form an image. The image is a conscious thought that communicates to the subconscious mind. The subconscious mind takes it as real, and, like a magnet, will draw everything you need to make it happen.

The trick is to keep the old paradigms from overpowering the new vision. This is the key to you creating the stage, the skinny jeans, the money—everything. Now remember, I *did* say it was simple, but you should also know that it's not easy. We don't overcome a pattern and then never have to deal with it again. Our patterns are always there, lurking in the background, waiting to be triggered. As we grow in our business and life, we will do things outside of our comfort zone. That is where our paradigms sit in wait and then, bam! They show up. It's necessary to continually practice the steps of transformation in your truth.

YOU MUST IDENTIFY YOUR VALUES

To speak authentically with confidence and sell with authority you must align everything you do with your core values. Speaking from any platform is most powerful when your top values shape the foundation of both how you speak and what you say. In other words, whether in business or life, stand for what you believe.

Values are a part of us. They highlight what we stand for. They represent our unique, individual essence. They guide our behavior, providing us with a personal code of conduct. When we honor our personal core values consistently, we experience fulfillment. When we don't, we are incongruent and are more likely to disconnect from others and ourselves. As business owners and professionals, we need to identify and live out our core values for our greatest personal satisfaction. Furthermore, core values help us determine our personal brand message and what makes us unique in the market. What makes you different from everyone else in your industry? The answer lies in knowing your core values. Be clear about what those are.

Values help you to dictate your personal involvement and alignment when you hit the stage or platform. We work best with people who are in alignment with our values. In my thirty years of selling, I could *make* anyone a buyer. I could convince them to buy! But convincing isn't the same as converting, which happens when you allow the prospect to find her own *yes*. The problem with convincing is that, even though you might close every deal, you don't necessarily want to work with everyone! I was stuck with clients who were not aligned with my core values. Do your best to convert clients but be sure your clients are in alignment with your core values.

When you speak to profit, you communicate what is important to you and your audience by knowing your values. The audience can clearly understand who you are and if you are aligned with them. Authenticity and value-driven content and actions influence overall buying behavior. Your core values influence how prospects see you and what you stand for. You want to connect to the people you work best with, and you do that through your values. Values inspire people to act. People take positive action because they aspire to connect with others who are aligned with their core values.

I used to watch *Food Network Star*, where contestants would compete for their own Food Network television show. Throughout the show, each contestant worked to discover his or her point of view (POV). Their star power was based on a sparkly personality to hook an audience on TV and a keen ability to convey a strong, simple message—the all-important culinary POV. Contestants would have to determine what story their food would tell to the viewing public. What is the story you will tell to your viewing public? What is your POV? What do you stand for?

Values inform your POV and allow you to authentically connect with the audience. One of my values is integrity. I believe in telling the truth and telling it quickly. When I am delivering a presentation from stage or any platform, I am upfront and tell all. Integrity is always important to me. Every year I hold a three-day event and provide content, training, and value to my audience. During the event, I make an offer for people to enroll in my programs. Unlike most speakers pitching at their own events, I disclose every component of my offer. I never use manipulative tactics like leading the audience to believe they are doomed without my program. Truth be told, buy or not, they will be okay. They may not have the support that I offer, but they will be *all right*. I have attended countless events that lead the audience to fear homelessness if they don't buy the magic bullet program. Integrity requires me to honor people in their resistance and to support them through it.

To help further clarify alignment with your core values, let's say you host your own event with sponsors, and one of your core values is standing against animal cruelty. You wouldn't bring on a cosmetic sponsor that tests its products on animals. Doing so would be out of alignment with your core values, and you would be sacrificing them for sponsorship funds. If one of your core values is family, you won't submerse yourself in work and neglect your family. If you do, you are out of alignment with your values, and I'm betting you are not fully satisfied or fulfilled in your work.

Running a business and speaking from any platform requires you to be confident in your POV. Countless *Food Network Star* contestants were eliminated because they could not stand confidently in their POV and own it. To identify and own your POV, you need to know your core values and principles. Here are some bold statements to help you make a stance, increase your power, and position yourself in your life and business. Take some time to think about and answer these questions authentically:

Work: What is my greatest contribution in the world? Of all the work I have done thus far, what do I feel will have the most impact?

_____

_____

_____

Relationships: What matters most to me? What attributes do I need to fully satisfy my relationship needs?

_____

_____

_____

Money and financial success:

What I value most about money is

_____

_____

_____

Money makes me feel

_____

_____

_____

Health and well-being: What is the most important aspect of my health? How am I responsible for tending to my well-being?

_____

_____

_____

Family: What legacy will outlast me on Earth? What will I leave behind for my family to remember and follow?

_____

_____

_____

Impact: Why am I here? What am I meant to do with the life I have been given?

_____

_____

_____

Now that you have answered these questions and made bold statements about yourself, it's time to walk through the four steps to discover what is truly important to you, your POV. Let's dive deeper into what you really stand for.

STEP 1: WRITE A LIST OF WHAT'S IMPORTANT TO YOU.

What makes you truly happy? When do you feel you are living life to the fullest? What fires you up? What pisses you off? What thrills you? Write a complete list of the happiest moments in your life. Discover clues as to what you think is important by pondering how you spend your time, what you talk and think about the most, and what you spend your money on. Add these to your list. Remember, this list is all about you and for you only. Be honest; don't censor yourself or include things you think you *should* write down. Keep writing until you can't think of anything else that is truly important to you.

STEP 2: TURN YOUR IMPORTANT LIST INTO A CORE VALUES LIST—YOUR POV.

Behind each important item lies a core value. For example, if you like hiking up the mountain on the weekend, a core value might be health, challenge, or adventure. Determine what the corresponding value is for each of the items on your *important* list.

STEP 3: DECIDE YOUR TOP FIVE CORE VALUES AND FLESH OUT YOUR POV.

Your list of core values may be long. Some values will overlap, like honesty and integrity. Decide which is more important and keep that one. You might need to do some research to determine which one fits you best. According to Dictionary.com, honesty means "the quality or fact of being honest; uprightness and fairness." Integrity means "adherence to moral and ethical principles; soundness of moral character; honesty." As you can see, the words have very similar meanings, yet they're different in their own right. If you find that honesty and integrity are top core values for you, which one fits you best? Keep comparing one to the other until you whittle down your list to your top five.

Further narrow your list by considering:

- What values are *essential* to your life?
- What values represent your *primary way of being*?
- What values support your inner self?

STEP 4: PRIORITIZE YOUR TOP FIVE CORE VALUES AND ANCHOR YOUR POV.

All five of your core values are important. To further anchor a strong POV, prioritize the values by ranking them from one to five. Once you've got your precious list, check in with yourself. Does the list feel right? Do the values sum you up accurately? If not, go back to Step 1 and start again. Being aware of your core values is a critical first step to understanding yourself better and improving your life. Ultimately, though, it's what you do with this knowledge that matters. My suggestion is to put your list of top five values where you can see them every day: on the wall, a notice board, a post-it, as a screensaver. Then, every day for a week, ask yourself, "Am I living my life in tune with my core values?" If not, ask, "What do I need to take a stand on and change?"

Test out your list often until you own your POV. Ask a few questions that test your top five list. (1) How do these choices make you feel? (2) Are they consistent with who you are? (3) Are they personal to you? (4) Are they consistent with your identity (be careful they don't belong to an authority figure or society)? It's only when you make changes in line with your core values that you will find more harmony and peace in your life. I stand for making a difference, love, integrity, freedom, and growth. What are your top five core values that allow you to own your POV?

Living according to your core values is the cornerstone to thriving. Be true to yourself and never settle or live according to what someone else wants for you. Be who you are no matter what, without compromising. Knowing your core values keeps you true to yourself and living in your POV every day, not just from stage. People say that I am the same off stage as on stage. I never change my core beliefs, opinions, or values for anyone. I am true to myself. That didn't happen overnight. It takes time, dedication to self-awareness, and commitment. You, too, can confidently set limits and boundaries that honor what you believe in and live with conviction according to your own core values.

CHAPTER 4

SHIFT FROM POSSIBILITY TO PREDICTABILITY

What is possible for you? Many people don't believe they can have anything they desire or dream of in this lifetime. Why? It all goes back to what we've been told and what we now believe to be true. I was a senior in high school when I started planning my future. In my last semester, I thought about going to college. I was not the most forward-thinking senior in my graduating class. Truth be told, I didn't believe I could go to college because of my thought habits and what others had told me. I presented my father with my idea to become an attorney, to which he responded, "That is for smart kids, and you aren't smart. You're kinda dumb." What he said felt accurate to me because I had been told that my entire life. I believed what I was told. It became my story. I didn't believe doing much of anything was a possibility that could become a predictability.

What story or belief holds you back? The good news is that, no matter the story or belief, you can create whatever you desire. You don't have to get rid of anything to live from possibility. Ask yourself, "What's going on for me in my current circumstances and conditions?" Move from possibility to predictability by doing three things: (1) Set your intention. (2) Think from possibility. (3) Manifest your desires.

SET YOUR INTENTION

Ralph Waldo Emerson said, "A good intention clothes itself with sudden power."[10] Merriam-Webster defines intention as "a determination to act in a certain way: resolve." My definition of intention is having in mind a purpose or plan, directing the mind, and aiming your actions in the right direction. Whether we know it or not, everything we do has an intention, good or bad. We do many things out of habit and routine. We go about each day intending to go to the store, to work, to play, and more. We automatically take action from the time we wake to the time we go to bed, but we don't always take intentional action. We don't always have a purpose or plan to direct the mind with right action. When we lack intention, we can stray without meaning or direction. But with good intention, all the forces of our efforts and actions align to make even the seemingly impossible possible. Intention is a way to transform thoughts from fear and doubt to possibility and then probability, coupled with action and results.

Start with the basics of intention, so that you can fully understand how your intention is vital to creating the business and life you desire.

Basic 1: Everything that we desire is already created in the physical. Our job is to be open to receiving it. In more than twenty-five years of studying mindset and the laws of life, I have learned that 99.999% of all we want in life already exists. Things are created twice, first in thought and then in form. So, think a thing and then be open to receive it because it is out there. The work is welcoming it into your life. I use the affirmation, "I am receiving, I am receiving, I am receiving now. I am receiving all the good life has to offer me." I recite this affirmation when I am walking. With every step, I say each word to myself.

Basic 2: What you are living right now is an indicator of your thoughts and beliefs. Everything you have or experience is an exact reflection of your thinking. If you want to know what you have been thinking, look around you. Your world reflects your thinking. If there's a mess in your surroundings, your thinking probably feels chaotic. If you are angry, you encounter angry people. If you have thoughts of not enough, your life manifests that as a reality. If you are making sales calls and you think no one will buy, no one will buy. The power of your thoughts is creating your current reality. Follow Henry Ford's wisdom—think you can and watch the rightness of that unfold.

Basic 3: Conditions, circumstances, or facts of our life are temporary. Things we think will never end do eventually end. Life is ever changing to the construct of our minds, our thoughts, and our intentions. Life is a momentary indicator that can be changed through our thinking and our conscious intention-setting followed by right action. What we think, we move toward. For example, if you are faced with bills and feeling stress about paying them, you can't easily focus on wealth. If you want to accumulate wealth and abundance, you can't think broke and complain about no money. They are two opposing intentional thoughts. When you catch yourself thinking negative thoughts, do your best to think a more positive thought in a very general way. For example, to shift thinking about being fat, the general way to think the opposite is to think about what you prefer. "I prefer to think I can possibly drop some weight." Or think of one thing that would change as a result of losing the weight. Go general in your thinking and wait to develop details until you are able to believe the desired outcome.

Basic 4: We live in an abundant world made up of all that we could ever hope for. Exercise your ability to receive the things you set your intention on. We each create our life, whether by default or by design, by setting good or bad intentions. Each one of us has the same amount of time: 365 days or 525,948 minutes every year. We create with each thought during those thousands of minutes. Look upon the infinite possibilities of your life and consciously choose. In the absence of conscious choice, we create unconsciously.

How do you use intention to your benefit? First and foremost, intention requires high participation and a low attachment to the outcome. It requires a focus on your desire and why you would love what you desire while suspending the need to know how. Guess what? *How* is none of your business! The logical mind has been trained to ask how or to figure things out based on the conditions or results. We want to know exactly what it looks like and what we need to do to get the results we want.

For example, if I have fifty dollars in my checkbook and the thing I want costs sixty dollars, I translate that into, "I can't get that thing." A person who has no college degree may believe her capacity for success is limited. These beliefs are based on what we see as fact. Here's the good news: facts can change. The fact is I live in Phoenix, Arizona, but the truth is I can move. The fact is I weigh 125 pounds, but the truth is I can gain or lose weight.

The foundation for your success is understanding the fundamental truths related to the power of intention. Begin with discovering the nature of you. By nature, you are creative. Creating is not optional; it's a given. Whether you buy into this or not, whatever you put your attention on, you create. You have the power to create good or bad. I love that I have the power to create good things, but I am not thrilled to experience the creation of bad things using that same exact power.

Your entire life is a result of your thinking. Thinking sets your intention, which is fueled by your attention. You get to describe how you want your life to be. Your attention, thinking, and emotions are like magnets, and they bring to you exactly what you think about, good or bad. When you put your attention on something, it becomes your intention, and the universe orchestrates an infinite number of events to materialize your desires. Your intention is a mold for the things you think about. You imagine the desire, and life fills it in. Intention is amazing! It lays the groundwork for effortless, spontaneous expression of what you want!

Intention works like this. You get an idea, which leads you to an image of what the idea would be like if it were a reality. Your image, in turn, generates a feeling, resulting in an action, inevitably creating a result.

Intention is the secret ingredient to generating success in any area of your life. But many people get an idea, and instead of creating an image, they go to the *how*. Focus on the *how* creates an automatic subconscious response. The subconscious mind, if uninterrupted, retrieves evidence of possibility. Many people get an idea and automatically hear the untrue stories or beliefs about themselves. The stories and beliefs are their unconscious automatic patterns. These patterns are either inherited or anchored through repetition or trauma. If you hear something enough times, you interpret it as truth.

My parents believed we were always one day away from losing everything. My mother was raised on welfare due to her alcoholic father losing the farm. My father, on the other hand, grew up with depression and a "lack" mentality. I heard repeatedly that we couldn't afford to spend money. As a result, my money story reflected my parents' beliefs. Their money stories became a pattern, my bad habit of thinking. We all have unconscious automatic patterns that get triggered. The key is to be aware of what we think, our self-talk, and the stories and beliefs about ourselves. These patterns affect how we set our intentions.

If you get an idea and your mind defaults to the belief that everything is hard or takes a ton of effort, then that thinking takes away your blank canvas to create a brand-new picture. Instead, your canvas is splattered with paint. You must overcome the color already there to create a beautiful new picture. Most of us love new ideas, and we get them often, but we also have a habit of thinking that prevents us from easily manifesting the results. You may, for example, have a story that you have to work hard for what you want or that you have to overcome conditions before you can be successful. No matter the evidence of your success in the past, your default pattern of thinking focuses on struggle, can't, and effort. Thought patterns are your knee-jerk reactions to ideas. My dear friend and mentor, Mary Morrissey, taught me that the best way to discover your default patterns is to "notice what you are noticing." Noticing helps us clarify your focus, which determines your intention.

What do you notice? Do you notice the lack in your life? Do you notice struggle or abundance? This is important when you are setting your attention. Stay in relationship and maintain an awareness of what you are focused upon. This will guide your interest and keep you on track. In absence of this guidance, you may be attracted to the random things that are not in alignment with your intention. Some people call this "shiny object syndrome" or "squirrelitis." You cannot believe you will have a wildly successful business when you focus on being broke. You cannot gain wealth by thinking thoughts of poverty. The only way to create wealth is to think and pay attention to wealth. Set your intention on exactly what you want, and that will focus your attention.

HOW TO SET INTENTION

I have studied the principles of intention setting for years. It sounds simple, but trust me, it is not easy. We have established beliefs that interfere with our new ideas and thoughts. It can be frustrating. There are three stages to setting intention: (a) build a relationship with your subconscious mind; (b) cultivate a clear channel for your intention and results; (c) create an image.

The **first stage** is to build a relationship with your mind, specifically the subconscious mind. The subconscious mind holds all our patterns of thought. Listen to your thoughts, especially your self-talk. Be aware! Notice what you are noticing.

The **second stage** is to open a clear channel for your intention and the results you wish to create. For example, if you are listening to CNN and you want to see what is happening on the Discovery channel, you need to change the frequency. You can't hear success on the channel that broadcasts failure. You cannot experience love on the frequency that broadcasts abandonment. Tune to the station that broadcasts your desired outcome. When you notice you are out of alignment with your desire or the frequency that broadcasts your desire, change the channel. You cannot change the channel unless you are aware of what is being transmitted. You cannot experience profound success if you are playing the wrong channel.

Get crystal clear about what you want in your life and business, so you can recognize when you need to change the frequency.

The **third stage** is to create an image. The image is not based on what we think we are capable of or what our conditions will allow. It's not based on past experiences, successes, or failures. Do not let your history predict your accomplishments. You are not your past. You are not what happened to you or what you have done. Do not let what is predicted in your life determine your future. Nothing predicts your results without your consent. You grant consent when you are not mindful of the frequency you listen to.

Intention requires a commitment to be in harmony with your desired outcome. You must practice more empowering thoughts and turn up the volume on possibility. What would you love to have happen in your life? What if all you had to do was set your intention and diligently focus on the positive thoughts around the results?

Try this intention-setting exercise.

1. Each day set your intention for overall outcome and for each event or activity that day.

2. Focus, meditate, pray, journal, get out in nature, and establish an auto-suggestion routine. Auto-suggestions are essentially affirmations. I call them auto-suggestions because, in my opinion, our minds have become desensitized with affirmations. Create auto-suggestions like this:

   a. "Imagine if _____
      _____."

   b. "What if _____ were possible? What would that look like?"

   c. "I am so happy now that I am _____
      _____."

    d. "I love that I am _____
    _____."

3. When you go to bed, repeat a positive statement one hundred times. I go to bed repeating, "I am prosperous" or "Everything is so easy."

The work is to discover and change our patterns of thinking so that they align with our intention. To change results, you must change your thinking. Begin to think from possibility.

THINK FROM POSSIBILITY

On August 5, 2005, I volunteered to work with the Phoenix Children's Project, a back-to-school program. I wanted to help a family in need and buy school supplies and uniforms for a few kids. I ventured into the housing projects of South Phoenix. Now, let me say that I'm not a big fan of kids that are—how do I say it—not accustomed to rules. I was the youngest of seven kids. My mother was like Captain Georg von Trapp from *The Sound of Music*. She ran a tight ship with a whistle and a ton of rules. After my trip to Walmart with two kids obviously unaccustomed to rules, I planned for a quick drop off. As I turned to make my fast exit, I bumped into a young African American boy who came up to my waistline. He was dressed in last year's school uniform, two sizes too small. His pant legs ended just above his socks, and his toes were wearing through the front of his shoes.

He greeted me with an ear-to-ear smile and an outstretched hand. As he took my hand in his, with a very solid grip and a professional handshake, he said, "My name is Darrol Robinson. I would like to know who you are and how I can get involved in this program. I would like to contact you to see how I can immediately start this program." At the time, Darrol was ten years old and being raised by his grandmother, who rescued him from an abusive and neglectful situation. Growing up with little to no emotional connection with his mother and never knowing his father, Darrol would be left for weeks in the care of his brother, who was only one year older than Darrol. No stranger to starvation, neglect, worry, fear, and horrific conditions, Darrol was the perfect candidate to become a horrible statistic. He was told he was too dumb to attend college. He was put into a school for kids with behavior disorders and aggressive tendencies. Automatic negative thoughts were programed into Darrol from the day he took his first breath. His view of his world was imprinted into his subconscious mind, and still he reached out to say, "I want in."

That day, Darrol's words, his smile, and those short undersized pants gripped my heart. Before beginning my speaking business, I had more than ten years under my belt working with and counseling kids, whether in prison, drug and alcohol treatment centers, or in the school system in prevention and interventions. The moment Darrol spoke to me, I saw something in this young man that compelled me to commit to nurturing his desire and passion to be more than he currently was.

To date, Darrol has not left my side. He is currently enrolled in college, works at the hospital as a security guard, works at the Boys and Girls Club as an activity leader, and is testing to become a Phoenix Police officer. He could have bought into the story and circumstances of his life, but instead, Darrol chose to speak up and play full out. How do you overcome your story or beliefs so that you can fully show up in your life?

MANIFEST YOUR DESIRES

You may be familiar with the language around the Law of Attraction, which is the name given to the maxim "like attracts like." This New Thought philosophy sums up the idea that by focusing on positive or negative thoughts, a person brings positive or negative experiences into their life. This concept is based upon the premise that people and their thoughts are both made from pure energy and that like energy attracts like energy.

Rhonda Byrne, claims in her book, *The Secret*,[11] that positive thinking can create life-changing results, such as increased happiness, health, and wealth. *The Secret* has sold more than nineteen million copies worldwide. Its basic premise is that the universe is governed by a natural law, the Law of Attraction, which is said to work by attracting into one's life the experiences, situations, events, and people that match the frequency of one's thoughts and feelings. From this, the book argues that thinking positively can create life-changing results, such as increased wealth, health, and happiness.

Is it true? Can the way we think make or break our success? Do we truly have the power to manifest our desires and have it all? For the last twenty years, I have studied and followed numerous teachings on how we have the power to manifest anything we choose. I have studied quantum physics, New Thought, scripture, Transcendentalism, Abraham Hicks, Thoreau, Wallace D. Wattles, Maxwell Maltz, Napoleon Hill, Joseph Murphy, Joyce Meyers, and many more. I refer to these teachings studies as the "Laws of Life." I would love to say that I can prove these laws don't work, and I do not have the power to create everything. I would love to blame certain circumstances and manifestations on someone or something other than my own thinking. But the power of the subconscious mind is undeniable. I firmly believe my thoughts are reflected in my outside world. Remember, your life is a perfect reflected reality of your thinking. If you want to know what you're thinking, look around you.

Why is this important? The Laws of Life collaborate with the subconscious mind. We can talk about, create affirmations, or plaster our mirrors with post-its stating our every desire, but if we have a different pattern of thinking running in the background, that pattern overrides all else. Our dominant thought, belief, or pattern creates our reflected reality. When I coach entrepreneurs, my primary beginning focus is to help them discover their money personality and their money story. We study the money patterns, beliefs, or behaviors they witnessed growing up that shaped their story about money and their relationship to money.

CHAPTER 5

REWRITE YOUR MONEY STORY

One of the most important things you can do to improve your financial situation is to understand your money story by identifying your existing relationship with money—what you say about money, how you feel about it, what you believe about it, and how you use it. You want to understand your feelings about money because your past experiences, emotions, thoughts, and beliefs drive your behavior, consciously and unconsciously. So, let's dive into your unique money story, starting with where it came from.

We inherit hair, skin, and eye color; hair type; finger and toe length; dimples; freckles; body type; height; hand dominance; mathematical aptitude; mannerisms; likes/dislikes; love/hate of foods; and our money story! Yes, we have inherited a pattern or story around money. The key to improving your money story is elevating or emphasizing the positive aspects of your story. Unfortunately, many of my clients give more attention to the negative aspects of their story.

My parents passed down their money habits and story to me. I grew up the youngest of seven kids in the Chicago area. My father had parents who survived the Great Depression. His family had money coming in but never wanted to spend any of it. Everything that the family purchased had to be earned or justified. My father grew up believing you must work hard for your money, and there is never enough to go around. His motto was, "Get your fair share and save it for a rainy day." My mother was the youngest of twelve children. Her father was an alcoholic, and he literally lost the farm. She and her family moved to a tiny apartment and lived on welfare. From the time she was fourteen years old, my mother worked to help support the family. She wore hand-me-down clothes including overalls that were two sizes too big.

I learned a few things from my parents around money that show up occasionally in my day-to-day business. One is my story that there is not enough to go around. As I watch others in the industry making far more money than I, I strive to work harder to get my fair share. Or I feel defeated and think there won't be enough to go around. It is exhausting when I am trying to work and the little voice in my head is reciting my money story. Another component to my money story is that there will never be enough. A part of me also believes that if you don't work hard constantly, your money will all go away. Please, don't let me be a bag lady! It might interest you to know that there is an actual Bag Lady Syndrome. The syndrome was first coined in the 1970s to describe the feeling some middle-aged women have that they'll wind up homeless and carrying around their possessions in shopping bags. For years, that thought lurked in the back of my mind and drove me hard in my business.

I discovered the driving force behind my success was my money story and my fear of losing it all. The problem with my money story is it took the fun out of everything. I worked from fear and not from the love of my work. Re-writing your money story will help you to be motivated and inspired by the love of your business and money, not by fear or dread. I want to emphasize the importance of understanding your motivating factors before you get to the point of burn-out or dissatisfaction in your work. Ask these questions to discover your money story:

1. Did your family experience a defining moment around money? Defining moments shape our beliefs around money. We take meaning from the experience. Do you recall a significant event

that may have caused the loss of family wealth, a job, living through the Recession, or a divorce that caused financial duress?

2. Did your family experience sudden wealth or financial success? If so, what did they do with the money? What were their thoughts and actions around this flood of wealth? How did your life change? How did they change?

3. What memories do you have of your parents discussing money? Did they argue about money, or did your parents have differing views on spending and saving?

4. What is your earliest memory about money?

5. Do you have unhappy childhood memories around money?

6. What emotions did your family associate with money?

7. How would you define the status of your family growing up? Were they considered rich, poor, or middle class?

8. Did your family's ethnic or cultural background affect your beliefs about money?

9. What was the attitude toward money of your family's church or religious tradition?

10. What are your unhappiest memories (from childhood or later) about money?

11. What are your happiest memories (from childhood or later) about money?

12. How do you feel about your current financial circumstances?

13. How would you describe yourself around money (generous, stingy, thrifty, extravagant, responsible, careless, etc.)?

14. How do you feel when you think about your financial situation and retirement or old age?

Now write one paragraph: My current story around money is

_____

_____

_____

_____

_____

_____

Now write one paragraph: My current relationship with money is

_____

_____

_____

_____

_____

MONEY PERSONALITY TYPES

The objective to further unfold your money story is to gain greater self-awareness, personal understanding, and a sense of emotional intelligence. A deeper sense of your motivating factors helps you control your thoughts and behaviors. It helps to know what you like and don't like, what you're good at, and what your challenges are around money. After all, money is the end result of the work we do in the world. If we want to sell with authority rather than desperation, then we must take command of our money fears and habits.

After researching spending styles and studying various money personality types, I have modified the personality types and applied them to entrepreneurs, sales professionals, and anyone offering a service or product. After thirty years of sales success, I've distilled it all down to four money personality types: (1) the Hoarder, (2) the Spender, (3) the Avoider, and (4) the Money Monk.

1) THE HOARDER

The primary focus of a Money Hoarder is to obtain security. People hoard money because they fear that if they make one false move or experience an unexpected disaster, all their money will be gone. Money Hoarders believe that no matter how much money they have, it's never enough. They deny themselves pleasure for fear they will waste their money. They're like squirrels, storing it away for when they "really need it."

You can recognize Money Hoarders by their behaviors. They enjoy saving money, and they carefully prioritize their financial goals. They budget faithfully, and their favorite pastime is creating and fine-tuning that budget. Spending money is difficult for Money Hoarders. They feel that spending money on entertainment and vacations is especially unnecessary. Their personal slogan: "Save for a rainy day."

When Money Hoarders invest money, it's all for the future. They keep a stash of cash in secret places in their home. They sneak their own popcorn into movies. They love watching the savings pile up or getting a great bargain and sharing with friends about their latest deals. Unfortunately, the Money Hoarder often doesn't grow her business as fast or successfully because she fears taking any risk. If you're a Money Hoarder in business, you resist spending money on an assistant, so you end up working twelve-hour days. You may not invest enough in yourself, and you tend to over worry and over work. You may suffer in order to save. Notice if you ever take the time to celebrate your success.

I relate only too well to the Money Hoarder. I have money stashed away, *love* to save, and hate to invest in building and paying a team. It started when I landed my first job out of college. Back in the day, we actually received a physical paycheck. My check came on the second week of the month. I would put my check in the center console of my car and leave it there until I got my next paycheck. I would rotate the checks out every two weeks and deposit them into the bank. I called it my forced savings plan. The checks would pile up sometimes, and I loved to feel the growth of my savings. To this day, when I receive a check, I let it sit for a week and enjoy the thought of putting it into my account. I am a Money Hoarder.

2) THE SPENDER

The Spender spends in order to feel important, loved, and validated. If you are a Spender, spending energizes you. The inner voice of a Spender says, "I deserve this. I won't be denied anymore. I am worth it." You can recognize Spenders by their behaviors. The biggest Spenders are status seekers who equate extravagant possessions with self-worth. Whether they can afford it or not, that Louis Vuitton bag makes them feel respected. Who cares if they have a closetful of handbags—they feel justified and deserving of that new Louis Vuitton bag! Money is meant to be enjoyed and to make life better. Spenders get a real kick out of buying things and services for their immediate pleasure. They love to wow their friends with fabulous gifts. They have difficulty saving money; therefore, it is a challenge to put aside enough to meet their long-term financial goals. The habit of spending too much money may cause an accumulation of debt, possibly significant debt. Spenders have never met a credit card offer they didn't like.

Unfortunately, the Spender tends to invest in too many certifications, programs, and trainings, but they have little return on their investment. They become addicted to investing and not accumulating wealth. The

Spender actually finds it fun to invest in new and exciting programs for self-enhancement with little or no financial return. In addition, Spenders are never fully satisfied and don't always find the answer they are looking for. They repeatedly take uncalculated risks.

I have witnessed Spenders attending events and throwing dollar after dollar on products and services, investing money they do not have and will not recover. I see the look in their eyes and hear them celebrate in their investments. They believe they have finally found the answer they have been looking for in their struggle. I don't deny there are solutions to help improve your business. My suggestion is to look at how much you have spent in the past and your return on investment. Spenders do not look at the return. They love to buy!

3) THE AVOIDER

The Avoider avoids at all costs (no pun intended) the subject of money. Identify Avoiders by their common behaviors. Avoiders procrastinate about dealing with finances and often don't even know how much is in their bank account. They avoid planning for retirement because it feels too far away to worry about. Numbers scare them or create stress, confusion, or frustration. Rarely do they stay informed about their finances. I confess that I hated looking at my numbers. It triggered worry and the feeling that I was not doing enough. I put undue pressure on myself and drove myself even harder. I trained myself to look at my numbers only when I was in the right frame of mind. I believed the best frame of mind is to eliminate attachment to the outcome. In other words, don't look at your numbers when you are feeling a sense of lack or unworthiness. It will destroy your motivation and momentum.

Furthermore, Avoiders miss opportunities to set the foundation for a more financially secure future. They may not pay their bills on time, and they put off doing their taxes until the last minute. Additionally, they typically don't make a budget or keep any kind of financial records. The result is that Avoiders have no idea how much money they actually have, owe, or spend. This causes a false sense of urgency to make money.

If some of these traits describe your money personality, the lack of knowledge frees the mind to fill in the blanks. For example, Avoiders whose money story says there will never be enough operate according to that fear. They have a tendency to overwork and over worry, because they don't know how much they truly need to make. They have no clue how many hours they need to work. It becomes a vicious cycle of avoid, work, and worry. They spend excessive energy *avoiding*. This can leave them feeling incompetent or just overwhelmed by money tasks. The subject of money paralyzes them. The less they know about their finances, the better.

4) THE MONEY MONK

The Money Monk fears giving in to the seductive power of money, or that she will become *one of those people*. Money Monks were raised with deep religious, political, or judgmental convictions that money is the root of evil, or that rich people are "capitalist pigs." They believe some things about money that cause them to avoid making too much. They believe money is dirty or that having money is not spiritual. They believe that having too much money will corrupt them and lead them to greed and selfishness. Many believe money is not very important and that it is a limited resource. The basic belief of the Money Monk is that money ruins you.

Money Monks are minimalistic and embrace a no-frills lifestyle. A very common trait of Money Monks is to make money and then give it away. They resist big money opportunities and criticize others who make a lot, calling them slimy, greedy, or *one of those people*. They are bargain hunters who rarely pay full price for anything. They sacrifice to make do. You may hear a Money Monk say, "The rich get richer, and the poor get poorer."

I had a friend in the lending business who began to make a significant amount of money. As she grew more and more successful, her mother said things like, "You better be careful, you will become one of those people." Her mother was referring to people who get greedy and take advantage of others. My friend's mother was a Money Monk.

In business, Money Monks will barter or trade for business and services. They give things away, they give deals and discounts, and they can't close the sale. They have a hard time saying no or setting boundaries. Their number one priority is to help others, and as a result, they put themselves last, even when they can't pay their bills. They simply give too much away and don't receive enough in return. This leaves them wondering why they can't make more.

WRITING AND LIVING A NEW MONEY STORY

Knowing your money personality type will help you write and live a new story about money. What type are you? You may be a combination of the various personality types. Determine which is your predominant type. Once you have narrowed this down, constantly be aware of when and if you are operating from this type. The faster you discover your money type, the sooner you create success. No matter your money personality or the story you tell about money, it is necessary to rewrite the existing story to create a new and more expanded one. If you keep telling your current money story, you will keep creating the same dynamics over and over again.

The success of the sales process depends upon your money type and an empowering money story. Think about it. If you give deals and fast discounts to buyers, you exhibit some degree of the Money Monk. This will affect your bottom line every time. If you are an Avoider and have no idea what is coming in and going out, you create excessive stress in your business and life. Running a business as the Spender gives you a ton of write-offs but will never make you rich. The key is to balance the spending and eventually bring in far more than you spend. More importantly, spend your money on smart products and services that guarantee a positive return. If you identify with the Hoarder, your new story is to celebrate and invest money wisely in your business and yourself.

Selling is the basis of your success. The game changer in your business is a new money story that will result in more conversions and closed deals.

Let's look at changing the story you've been telling about money by using my three-step Rewrite Your Money Story process: (1) Change your money expression. (2) Change your money perception. (3) Live your new money story. This process will help you identify daily behaviors and habits that you do unconsciously. You will start to notice what you do that keeps the old story alive. After completing this process, you will better understand why sales fall apart or fade away. Rewriting your money story helps you to create a new way of operating in your financial world. Know that old behaviors and habits will not go away overnight. Pay vigilant attention to the steps in the process and catch yourself when you slip into old habits.

CHANGE YOUR MONEY EXPRESSION

The first step to rewriting and living a new money story is to change your verbal expressions about money. What do you tell people about money and your relationship to it? Identify what you regularly tell people about you and money. Write these statements down. For each statement, write a more empowering expression. For example, if you say repeatedly, "I never have enough money," a more empowering statement might be, "I know there is plenty of money in the world, and I will attract my desired amount to me." A statement so directly opposite to your habitual language will trigger a niggling retort that you will never make it beyond your current financial status. WHEN, not if, that happens, simply write another statement to combat this thinking.

For example, a more believable statement might be, "I might not have evidence of the desired flow of money, but I see living proof in the world that money is flowing. If other people can do it, maybe I can as well." As you can see, subtler statements ease the mind into a new story. If you go too fast, your mind will reject the new thought, and you cannot work your way into the new story. In other words, you cannot go from seeing a hundred dollars in your checking account to believing a story that shows two million dollars in your account. Your mind will reject any possibility of those millions becoming a reality, so you will feel defeated before you even get started.

CHANGE YOUR MONEY PERCEPTION

The second step to rewriting your money story is to change your perception of money, to see money differently. People have very different perceptions about money and what money can do. How can you change your relationship to these common perceptions about money? Write a list of ways you can be of service to others when you have money. How would having more money improve your life, your family, and the world? Next, write a list of wealthy role models who make a difference with their money. Create a vision of the things you would do to share the wealth. Is it a list of charities you could support? Is it a family you could help?

My list consists of randomly paying off people's medical bills, homes, and cars. In addition, I would purchase acreage and have a rescue ranch for dogs and horses. I would open a shelter for sexually abused girls, providing support and love for them as they heal and grow. What will you do?

LIVE YOUR NEW MONEY STORY

The third step is to live your new money story even before it is here. That means living as if you have the money you desire. Start by surrounding yourself with people who have money! Maybe you've heard that we become like the top five people we most associate with. Let go of people who complain about being miserable or broke. Beware of the naysayers, those who doubt any dream or vision you have for your life. Thoughts, actions, and attitudes are contagious. Hang around possibility thinkers.

Motivational speaker Jim Rohn famously said that we are the average of the five people we spend the most time with. This relates to the law of averages, which theorizes that the result of any given situation will be the average of all outcomes. When it comes to relationships, we are greatly influenced—whether we like it or not—by those closest to us. They affect our way of thinking, our self-esteem, and our decision-making. We all need people—cofounders, mentors, family, or friends—to challenge us and make us better. The right circle raises our average or helps us maintain a higher bar. Some entrepreneurs strive to be the smartest person in the room on every issue. But you will benefit more by surrounding yourself with people who can run circles around you in multiple areas, people who are exponentially better in a variety of ways.

No, this doesn't mean dump anyone in your life who isn't making money. But it *is* vital to relate to them in a different manner. Strive to collaborate with individuals by mentoring up, and hang out with people whose setpoint is wealth, prosperity, and possibility. Create an environment that is conducive to wealth and abundant thinking. Identify what conversations, people, or situations support your money desires. Also, be aware of the conversations, headlines, or comments you notice most. When you notice continuous talk about a poor economy, increased unemployment, or other equally bleak topics, change what you're paying attention to. As I always say, the world is a reflected reality. What we see in the outside world is a perfect reflection of our inside world. Your dominant thinking shows up in the conversations you have, the people you meet, and the focus of your attention.

What happens if you find yourself transmitting from the frequency of lack? I recall years ago noticing people arguing. It seemed I was constantly surrounded by angry people. That experience was the perfect reflection of my inner world. I was doing some deep healing in my therapy, and I was mad about it! Apparently, I didn't allow myself to express my own anger, so the world reflected my feelings back to me. That experience allowed me to accept and deal with my feelings in a healthy, productive way. Out with the old and in with the new. I began to focus on a happy me, and the world began to reflect that back perfectly.

Let's start by doing an experiment with your money story. Set a BOLD money goal, so that your thoughts are equally bold and obvious. I want to shake it up a bit. If you set a goal that is uncomfortable enough, you will discover the hindering thoughts and feelings you have as a reaction to the goal. For example, when I first started my real estate business, I only landed the $150,000 listings. I saw other agents taking $500,000 listings, but not me. When I thought about it, my system rejected that it was even remotely possible. I had a number of thoughts contradicting the goal of anything above $150,000. I began to track those thoughts, which were key to expanding my thinking and believing. I knew that to achieve anything, I needed to change my thinking.

You, too, may need to change your thinking. Most of us do. Trust me, I have studied these principles for more than twenty years, and I still catch myself thinking contrary to my desires. It takes practice and noticing. So, when you set a money goal, keep track of the thoughts that run through your mind. Journal the various stories you tell and watch what the world is reflecting back to you. This exercise is less about obtaining the goal and more about harnessing the power of your thinking. Your automatic thoughts and patterns that run in your mind affect all areas of your life. When you track the beliefs and patterns that rule your outcomes, you can transform them into a new way of thinking.

American author Napoleon Hill was one of the earliest producers of the modern genre of personal success literature. In chapter twelve of his classic *Think and Grow Rich*, Hill says, "TRULY, Thoughts are things, and powerful things at that, when they are mixed with definiteness of purpose, and burning desire for their translation into riches or other material objects."[12] Your mindset creates your reality. It controls and influences your actions, choices and behaviors, all of which are important in pursuing and achieving any goal. This is why, if you want to experience greater levels of wealth, you need to think differently. Your current thinking has created your current life experience. Ask yourself, "What would I have to think about myself and who do I have to BE in order to earn my desired income and live the life of my dreams?"

Think differently and, at the same time, have definiteness of purpose and a burning desire. WHAT? How is one expected to do all of this and run a business, household, and life? I get it. It sounds complicated, but if you diligently pay attention to your thoughts, you will gain a greater understanding of your current patterns. Start by turning off the TV, radio, news, or any other noises that distract you from your thinking. Your thoughts are the key to your success. When you eavesdrop on the mind chatter, it's easy to counteract the messaging. You need to know what your current thoughts are to change them and think differently. So, reduce the external noise and distractions.

Thinking differently requires taking time to actually think. Our minds are on autopilot and constantly active. Thinking means intentionally using the mind to reason or consider something. Develop the ability to *automatically* think differently. Most of us operate from a consistent habit of thought. Only when we intentionally think differently will we get different results. Set a timer for every hour on the hour to deliberately think. Decide what you want to think about. Think about it for no more than five minutes, but focus on your intentional thought for the entire time. This activity builds willpower. Willpower means deliberately ignoring distractions while staying focused on the task at hand. The practice of deliberately focused activity forms a mental habit that soon will become your dominant thinking style.

Gaze at a candle flame to focus the mind. Or look at a dot on the wall. Focus all your attention on the flame or the spot. Using willpower to stay laser focused conditions the muscle of your mind. Meditate. Not only does meditation keep you calm and focused, research has shown again and again that mindfulness meditation can significantly boost attention span. In their "Brief Summary of Mindfulness Research," Greg Flaxman and Lisa Flook, Ph.D. demonstrate just how profoundly mindful meditation can influence your results in all areas of your life.[13] Researchers' interest in mindfulness practice has steadily increased as studies continue to reveal its beneficial effects. Current research looks at how the brain responds to mindfulness practice, how relationships benefit, and how physical and mental health improves

These studies help to further understand and see how when you increase your attention on your desired thoughts, your results improve. You don't have to spend all day meditating to get results. Ten to twenty minutes of meditation daily will do the trick. What's more, you'll enjoy greater clarity in your thinking after just four days.

To increase your power to focus on goals, start the morning by focusing for a few minutes on the breath. In addition to dedicating ten to twenty minutes a day to mindfulness meditation, experts recommend practicing mindfulness throughout the day. Mindfulness means focusing completely on what you're doing, slowing down, and observing all your physical and emotional sensations in that moment. Practice mindfulness when you eat by deliberately chewing your food thoroughly and concentrating on flavors and textures. Practice mindfulness when you apply lotion: smell the lotion; note the pleasure of smoothing a warm cream to your body; be aware of the sensation on your skin. Incorporating short sessions of mindfulness into the day will strengthen and expand your ability to think differently and intentionally. Mindfulness also helps dispel distractions as they arise. If you're working on a task and feel that restless itch to go do something else, bring your attention to right here, right now. Focus for a few seconds on your breath and notice how the distraction dissipates. Now you're ready to get back to work.

As an entrepreneur, I have lots of ideas all day long. These ideas can distract me from the task at hand. Strengthening the ability to focus on one thing at a time produces more satisfying results and leaves you feeling energized. Not only does thinking differently produce the results you want, but those results come with far less effort.

The bottom line: it's just as easy to think yourself across the world as it is to think your way across the room. If I ask you to imagine yourself on the beach in Hawaii, it would take you a fraction of a second to be in your speedo, on a towel, with your frozen drink in hand complete with one of those little fancy umbrellas. That's no more time than it takes to imagine yourself standing at the kitchen sink with the water running.

Thoughts are things. Think a thing and you can experience it in your imagination instantly. Once you imagine something, that thing is on its way to you. Are you open to receive? "Of course, I am!" You say. But the only reason we don't have everything we desire is because we are not truly open to receive. It isn't that we don't want to be open; it's that our resistant thought and belief are more powerful than our receptivity. I cannot stress this enough: our patterns, stories, beliefs, and paradigms fight for their lives. It takes effort and consistent persistence to incorporate a new way to think and be.

I started working on my thinking in 1990 when I was so frustrated with my conditions that I had to do something. I studied anything and everything from Sanyona Roman's *Living with Joy* to Napoleon Hill's *Think and Grow Rich*. I wanted to redefine my life. That required me to jump head first into teachings that would guide me through the obstacles of my mind. My stories and self-talk put up a fight every time I tried to step into a new way of being. That's where persistence came in. I was determined to overcome my inherited thought patterns and habits. In addition, I was committed to keeping my head above water financially.

Creating a consistent flow of financial abundance and wealth starts with receiving. Receiving is easier when you look at the basic laws of life, starting with the Law of Circulation. Everything is continuously circulating. What you give to someone, you will get back. It might come from a different source, but it will come back to you. That is the Law of Circulation. Life literally mirrors back to you what you do for others. We tend to keep score of what we give and what comes back. When we are locked into getting back from a specific source, we miss the flow that can come from a different source. As a result, we feel gipped, cheated, or shortchanged.

The best example of this was my father's "Birthday Club." He would send a card and a check for twenty-five dollars to my siblings and their family members on their birthdays. Very nice gesture! At least until someone didn't follow up with a timely thank you. Dad's unspoken rule was that if you didn't say thank you in his timeframe, next time you would receive only a card, no check. The next infraction reduced your gift to nothing. Don't get me wrong. Good manners are important and *thank you* is polite. But when we do things expecting something in return, we pinch off our flow of goodness. If you feel the need to receive something in return for your gift, reflect on your motive and intention. This awareness is vital to your flow and your ability to receive.

I learned this lesson when talking to Mary Morrissey on the phone. She asked me for a favor. I was willing to do anything for her. I said, "Of course! And in return, would you be willing to send me the song 'Bound Together'?" I was surprised at her response. It profoundly changed forever my giving mindset. Mary said, "Jane, either you want to do the favor or not. To freely give, there can be no conditions or strings attached. If you give to get in return, you create resistance in the flow of your good. I want our giving to be free from condition and open to great abundance, so give from the heart, and I will do the same." WOW! I won't lie. At first, I felt hurt and offended. Then my feelings passed, and I reflected on the gift of her conversation. I had been carrying an even-exchange mentality. "You give to me, and I will give to you in return." The old saying goes, "You scratch my back; I'll scratch yours." I never knew it was a conditional relationship. Thanks to my new awareness, I now give without expectation of return. I try always to be aware of my intention, yet I am far from perfect. Sometimes after the fact I realize that I have a little string attached. When our thinking is conditional, we create delay, resistance, or complete rerouting of our good.

In his book *Working with The Law*, Raymond Holliwell states, "When we relax from strain, the law has a chance to reply to our desires."[14] We work so hard to get what we want that our good doesn't have a chance to arrive. I tend to measure my return every step of the way. My expectation for results and what Holliwell calls "my strain" keep my good from coming to me. Have you ever focused intensely on something and then finally gave up on it? And once you gave up, did that thing you desire suddenly show up?

It showed up because when you gave up, you relaxed from strain, and the law had time and an open channel to respond to your desires. To be open to receive, we must allow and relax. Easy to say; not always easy to do.

In chapter eleven of *The Science of Getting Rich*,[15] Wallace Wattles discusses "Acting in a Certain Way." He is a master at simplifying our efforts for results. I recommend doing what I did to get results by daily reading chapters four, seven, eleven, and fourteen for ninety days. See for yourself, "THOUGHT is the creative power, or the impelling force which causes the creative power to act; thinking in a Certain Way will bring riches to you, but you must not rely upon thought alone, paying no attention to personal action. That is the rock upon which many otherwise scientific metaphysical thinkers meet shipwreck—the failure to connect thought with personal action."

Wattles wrote his book in 1903. Can you even believe it? This "thinking stuff" has been around a long time. He states his ideas in a simple way. I love it. I interpret Wallace Wattles' theory about "Acting in a Certain Way" to mean two different things. First, I think he means to demonstrate confidence and knowingness—to be certain. It means doing what you know will create the results you want to achieve. For example, when you go on a date, you act in a certain way. If you deliver a keynote, you act in a different certain way. You expect the way you act to generate desired results.

The other way I interpret "Acting in a Certain Way" is acting as if whatever you intend is done—as if the result is a given, and you know it implicitly. Acting with certainty is being faith-filled. Doubt, fear, and worry don't even cross your mind. I go to bed at night with certainty that I will wake up in the morning. I am not always certain how I will wake up. Occasionally, I get up on the wrong side of the bed, but I have no doubt that I will wake up. I am certain that my dogs will always love on me. Acting with certainty is powerful. It takes work and connecting to your higher power, whatever or whoever that may be. Your faith and knowing from that power relieves stress and strain. This transformational habit is the best way to allow the Law of Circulation and other laws of life to work on your behalf.

When we give in order to get, we are not "Acting in a Certain Way" or trusting that we will receive our good. Activating the Law of Circulation requires giving. (Tip: do not give despite yourself. Give when it is a resounding *yes,* and don't give when it is a definite *no.*) Lock onto the idea of giving. When we give our best—forgetting about ourselves and going the extra mile—money, success, love, and life flows generously. Everything has its opposite: hot and cold, up and down, day and night. We simply cannot receive if we do not give.

Is there a right and wrong way to give? I believe giving should be purposeful and free because if we give carelessly, we don't set the intention for a positive return. When we give to help those who help themselves—without strings attached—it comes back in a positive way. If we give in pity, our gift is actually a disservice to the receiver—not that they don't need what we have to offer, but because we are giving with negative energy. Let me explain further. We need to give and invoke the Law of Circulation. The Law of Circulation is the flow of energy that we put out into the world. It's the belief that what we give is what we can expect to receive.

I live in downtown Phoenix, Arizona. Occasionally, I encounter addicted homeless people asking for money. In good conscience, I cannot give them money. I believe they will drink or drug it away. Abiding by the Law of Circulation, I am in integrity only when I give to those who are willing to help themselves.

My clients pay me a fee to help them speak with confidence and sell with authority. In exchange, I give them my knowledge, experience, and coaching to help them achieve and surpass their success. They are appreciative, and I give with my heart, soul, and brain. Give only with a free and willing spirit without obligation or attachment. Otherwise, what returns comes with obligation or attachment. What you give, you get in return.

Make full use of your energies, faculties, and talents through useful giving. An open and unconditional attitude towards giving is not the bartering of the gift. Giving always precedes and predetermines the reception. Willingly give and graciously receive. When you give, you will receive. We are programmed to be "go-getters." I say alter this program and become a "go-giver," an idea that Bob Burg and John David Mann explain more about in their series of books about go-givers. Dr. Ivan Misner coined the phrase, Givers Gain®.[16] I agree. Givers create success from the inside out. Acting in a certain way helps you to be open to receive, as does giving unconditionally.

To increase anything in your life requires an unrestricted ability to receive. It is imperative to increase your ability to think and receive bigger and better. Most people increase incrementally; for instance, establishing financial goals for the upcoming year that are only a slight increase over the current year. I am not sure where we learned that we need to do things in stages, but I suspect Corporate America as one driver, conditioning us to the idea that increase is based on the "cost of living." Receiving only the standard increase each year develops an incremental mindset. There is nothing wrong with this method of increase. I simply suggest that we can develop the ability to receive that frees us from the limitation of incremental growth.

It's common knowledge that we must learn to walk before we can run. What if we didn't? What if we could just get up and sprint? What if, as we were rolling around drooling with our Binky™, we were told, "Very soon you will go from crawling to running. It is easy, and it's the most natural way for you to transport yourself from this toy to the next." This feels ridiculous and not even possible. But what if it were natural and normal?

Have you watched Discovery? They show baby elephants, deer, calves, long-horn sheep, or bison walking within hours after being born. It's a natural ability for the sake of survival. I am pretty sure that, if I might be eaten alive as I'm taking my first steps, I would be motivated to run for my life. Are you willing to run instead of walk into a financial windfall? Are you willing to do the inside work on your money story, beliefs, and the way you receive? Your willingness and intention will determine the degree and velocity of your success.

PART 2

SHOW UP

CHAPTER 6
COMMAND YOUR POWER

In Part 1: Speak Up, my focus was on you creating a business and a life that is fulfilling and satisfying. This required identifying your core values, telling your money story, and learning to think differently. Each new awareness has given you the necessary tools to speak with confidence and sell with authority. Now it's time to compile all the work you've done in the previous chapters into a message and talk that sells. But first, I want to set you up for success from any platform, whether it be on a stage, podcast, radio, video, or television. In doing so, I'll risk the assumption that most people have some degree of fear when speaking.

Statistics about the fear of public speaking abound. Generally, my experience tells me about ten percent of the population loves public speaking. People in that group experience no fear and get a huge high being in front of a large crowd. I am one of that ten percent. I love speaking, and I get high from being in front of any audience.

Another ten percent are genuinely terrified. Those people are physically debilitated by even the thought of public speaking. Glossophobics, those who fear public speaking, will go to great lengths to avoid speaking to a group. They experience nausea, panic attacks, and extreme anxiety. Heidi is one of my clients who displayed glossophobic tendencies. The first time I met Heidi, tears ran down her face. She was in full panic mode. She expressed her extreme fear of speaking and her need to overcome that fear if she was to be successful at her new coaching and consulting business.

She was a mess. Heidi didn't believe in herself. She felt that if she were to even get near a stage she would die, literally. She was unable to command her internal confidence and power. That lack of command would result in failure from any platform. Heidi represented the ten percent who hate public speaking.

The remaining eighty percent hover in the middle. These people experience butterflies, get anxious, don't sleep much the night before, but they know that they're going to live through it. It's just not much fun. Here's the good news: with a little work and few simple tools, you can turn those butterflies to your advantage and command your power.

Speaking with confidence and commanding power from stage is crucial to delivering your point to the audience. I have listened to speakers who have great content, but their delivery is weak—weak in the sense that they don't command power and authority over their subject matter. Move your audience into action by demonstrating your expertise. Someone once told me that I only need to know two percent more than my audience. At the time, I wasn't confident, and for crying out loud, I was in no way commanding. The two percent rule allowed me to gain a feeling of power over my audience. I decided I would experiment with it while delivering a talk to a room of fifty real estate professionals. I opened my talk with my usual WOW factor, a part of my talk formula you will learn in the upcoming chapter. I followed up with two questions: (1) Do you know my oldest sister's birthday and middle name? (2) Do you know what high school I graduated from and what year? The audience looked confused, and I said, "Thank goodness! It is widely known that a speaker only needs to know two percent more than her audience in order succeed. Phew, the pressure is off!"

The two percent tip helped me gain confidence and command my audience. If you want to move people to buy or act, you need to command your power both on and off stage. This requires work on expressing yourself and setting some limits and boundaries. You might be thinking, "I just want to speak and grow my business or my movement." I get it! But speaking is not just delivering some information and hoping people will buy. It is speaking with confidence and *knowing* people will buy.

It took me years to find my power, let alone command it. I started to practice commanding my power when I was in my early twenties. It wasn't pretty. I was downright clumsy. I knew I needed to stand up for myself more often and speak up for what I wanted. For the most part, I didn't say what was on my mind. I went along with the crowd or disappeared into the crowd. I held everything inside until I reached my boiling point. I was waking up inside but didn't know how to express it on the outside. I worked on it slowly but surely. The problem was that I built up resentments towards others because I felt taken advantage of or discounted. I was a doormat, and I grew tired of not being heard.

Almost overnight I went from being a doormat to a lion. Roar! I'd tear your head off, or I would cry. There was no in-between. Years ago, I suffered from irritable bowel syndrome (IBS), which was no surprise given the fact that I never spoke up. IBS required special dietary needs. When I went out to eat, I ordered much like Sally from the movie *When Harry Met Sally*. "I don't want this. Take that off. Put that on the side." Friends made fun of me, and I got very defensive. I roared at them: "I can't help it. I have to order like this, so knock it off." I went away crying, "Why do people pick on me?" I felt like the weakest cub in the pack. As if my food issues weren't enough, I have been a non-drinker since my freshman year of college. That was especially tough when we all would go to the bar. Everybody would comment about me not drinking. I'd say, "How is it a problem for you that I don't drink?" or I'd throw some profanity their way. I was very defensive and didn't command my choices. That left me with no power.

After numerous dinners and nights out at the bars, I finally said silently to myself, "It's okay to have my preferences." Once I gave myself permission to be however and whoever I wanted to be, I could accept and speak up for myself. I had made it wrong to want, need, or desire things. I began to be okay with myself and okay with people asking me questions or making comments, even teasing me. I owned my preferences and my power. Now I know what I want, and I express it. What I say and what I do demonstrate what I prefer. I let go of everyone else's opinions. Often, the people whose opinions are loudest are the ones not standing in their own truth.

I learned to command my power and not only have an opinion but own it. I became more confident and self-assured in my preference. You, too, will benefit by owning the power of your decisions. Make your yes be yes and your no be no. You can always change your mind. Just don't be lukewarm in your decisions. Think about how many times you say "yes," "no," or "I don't care" about even the simplest things. When someone asks if you want to go to a particular restaurant, notice if you respond, "no," "yes," or "I don't care." Awareness of your habit of response will reveal whether you do or don't speak up and voice your opinion. If you say "yes" when you mean "no," or if you regularly say, "I don't know," that's your cue to work on being stronger about who you are, what you want, and commanding your power. Everything you do will translate to the stage. That's why I teach people to speak up for themselves. Believe it or not, the way you do anything is the way you do everything.

If you have trouble asking for what you want, selling from the platform will be challenging as well. Ask for invitations to go to events, ask for help with a project you haven't been able to finish on your own, or ask for a sale. Practice asking for what you want. It's important to communicate clearly and ask. Remaining quiet and making people guess about what you want serves no one. Instead, speak up! Announce your preferences, guidelines, and expectations, and no one will be disappointed or surprised by what you say or do.

I am famous for having rules, boundaries, and strong preferences. I have worked on being direct (with love) and expressing my yes and no with clarity and timeliness. I even set up some guidelines for my coaches to include "xoxo" at the end of their email messages. I love x's and o's, so I ask for them. And guess what? People give them to me, and I do the same in return! I learned early in life that it is no one's fault but my own if I'm unhappy or unfulfilled. We each need to take responsibility for our own care and happiness. Start asking and ask often for what you want. Trust me, it will come in handy every time you want to make a sale or move people into action.

Communicate your preferences and limits by opening with, "Let me teach you about me," or "Let me help you understand me better." Paint a picture of your preferences for the other person. Believe me, you will get, "Ah-ha's!" and gratitude from people for letting them know who you are and what you really want. It takes the guessing out of relationships. As you can imagine, I am big on communication. If I have an issue and need to vent, I make sure that I help my listener know exactly what I need from them. The best example is calling my sister Mary for support. I tell her what I would love. Sometimes, I ask her if she would just take a moment to *hate* someone with me. I confess, when I get mad, I want my sister to support me by hating the person I am mad it. I know it's immature, but it works. If I let myself to go to the extreme of hating, I come back faster to understanding and healing. My sister is always willing to support me until I am over the hate. Now *that* is a truly loving and dedicated sister, and I love her for that. She has been my rock, hating and loving others at my request. I encourage you to find your Mary and ask that person to support you in any way you need.

You are the only one who knows what you want and what you need from other people. Practice expressing yourself with confidence. You will enjoy greater results in all that you do. This is the exact formula for speaking to profit. Authentically asking others to act is equivalent to asking your prospective clients to invest throughout your talk. You will develop a natural, strong delivery and close the deal. No matter how noisy, how much commotion, or how many distractions people hear in the world (online or offline), when you speak authentically, people listen. When you speak your heartfelt message, the world quiets down. When you are genuine, you can monetize what you're saying and what you do for people. It all starts with you finding your voice and commanding your power.

The power of your voice and how you express yourself will become all too clear for you, as it did for me when I was standing on stages early in my speaking career. There is nothing like a speaking evaluation or crowd reaction to trigger insecurities and lack of power. As a young speaker, I thought that I had to please and satisfy everyone in the audience. *Impossible!* Don't get me wrong, I am a very good speaker, but no one, not even the best of the best, will get a perfect ten for every performance. There is always that *one* person, and that person would get me every time. I would spot him right away and do my best to win him over. I depleted my energy and efforts due to my lack of self-confidence. I was not commanding my power; I was giving it away. The same insecurities played here as when I had to special order in front of my friends. Successful speaking requires owning your expertise, knowledge, and experience.

The 20-60-20 rule is a long-lived theory in the speaking world that saved me from bombing from stage. The rule states that in every audience twenty percent of the listeners won't like you much, twenty percent of the audience will love you no matter what you say, and sixty percent can go either way. I love those odds! If you can sway sixty percent of the audience, you are on your way to great success. You don't even have to worry about that *one* person, because you have so many others to work with. Knowing this theory allowed me to look for who loved me and not for who didn't. I found my *tribe* and spoke to them. Surprisingly, in doing so, I often swayed not only the remaining sixty percent, but even the other twenty percent who weren't supposed to like me. I still get that *one* person who keeps me from scoring a perfect ten, but now it doesn't matter.

From the stage, I progressed from merely suggesting ideas to directing the audience to implement the teachings and strategies I delivered. I took a position of power and authority. As a sales expert and professional speaker, I trust that my years of experience have given me some great tips that work. I challenge people to act on these tips. For example, in my talk formula, I teach you always to start with a WOW factor and never to start with thank you for having me. I know that starting a presentation that way loses you money. I have seen it happen time after time. Command your power and own your expertise.

Successful speaking shows off your life's accomplishments. Speak to a live audience by recorded video, or as part of a media interview. When people interview me, I love sharing who I am and what I do. Let's be honest, we all like to talk about ourselves. For me, it's an opportunity to be candid about what I do and why I am the best. And it helps me to serve more people. Few people in the world are willing to stand in their power and own their brilliance. During an interview, I get to share my insights and success to gain exposure and visibility. It's fun, and I believe I have earned it. You, too, have earned a place on the platform. You have a message, secret, formula, or genius to share, so share it!

Don't get me wrong, if you're ego-driven, that is a turn off. Showing off is about being authentically motivated and driven by the work you do in the world. You are the only one who can do what you do, so speak up and show it off! The best way to show off is to speak. This book delivers abundant information to help you step fully into your power, command that power, and ultimately command the stage. Now all you need is a talk. Phew! You are now ready to put your whole self into your talk and shake it all about. Your talk is the vehicle by which the world hears and sees you fully. More importantly, it's the vehicle to make you money.

CHAPTER 7

SPEAK TO PROFIT WITH YOUR SIGNATURE TALK

Speaking, no matter what venue or medium, is selling. So, how do you inspire others to take action that will benefit them? By speaking. And the delivery of your talk will either move them into action or not. Bottom line: you are selling someone on an idea and committed to having him or her take action. Sales gets a bad rap because we associate it as taking from someone rather than giving them the opportunity to do what they might think they cannot do.

Your responsibility as a speaker is to help people see what is possible. In other words, you help people initiate change in their lives and their businesses. Speaking is your vehicle to share your wisdom. You are always speaking, whether to an audience of one or one thousand, for seven seconds or seven hours.

You're about to create a unique signature talk that serves and *sells*. You have a unique message, and it is your responsibility to share that message and reap the reward of your brilliance. A significant part of that responsibility is to be a resource for your listeners. You will design a talk that gives your listeners information through rich content, emotional connection, relevant stories, and an invitation (aka "offer"). You will design and develop a signature talk that not only makes sales conversations easy and fun, but also brings you more client closure. Shall we begin?

There are eight steps to creating your talk.

1. Begin with the end in mind.
2. Start with your WOW factor.
3. Position me.
4. Position them.
5. Promise.
6. Provide content.
7. Call to action.
8. Close.

1) BEGIN WITH THE END IN MIND

First and foremost, begin with the end in mind! Where do you want to take the audience? What is the desired outcome? Your primary goal is to make a difference and to be of service, both to your audience and to yourself. You are in business; therefore, you want to make money delivering your message. Speaking is a lead-generating activity. Treat it as such. Create the offer or identify your desired outcome before crafting the talk. Your talk will lead the audience down the path to the outcome you design. Speak to sell, using your message effectively and authentically as you move your ideal clients to *yes*!

Let's reverse engineer your talk. Laser in on where you want to lead your audience, and then create powerful content. Ask these key questions to identify the end result you desire:

- What do you want your audience to **think**?
- What do you want your audience to **feel**?
- What do you want your audience to **do**?
- What do you want your audience to **receive** or to **buy**?

2) WOW FACTOR

Once you know where you will take the listener, the next step to create a big impact and a big outcome is to pull out your "WOW factor." The WOW factor is your opener, and it must demonstrate that you are not just any ordinary speaker. You have a matter of seconds to capture the audience's attention. The WOW factor is an unexpected beginning to your presentation. Your audience will expect you to begin like most speakers, thanking your host and introducing yourself. There is plenty of time for that. To command attention, start with a bang. This new way of opening will surprise and delight your audience.

I have a number of clients with immense talent. Two clients in particular, Darcy and Molly, have amazing singing voices. Both of these women have performed on big stages. I suggested using their talent for their WOW factor. Both of them open their talks with a short burst of song. The audience is amazed and captured every time.

Your WOW factor can be a song, a story, a quote, a statistic, an improvisation, role play, or something unique that engages the audience's attention. Remember, *never* begin with "My name is . . . " or "I'm glad to be here." You only get one chance to make a first impression, so save the pleasantries for later. I collect short stories, jokes, and statements to use as WOW factors. One way to find your WOW factor is to hop on the Internet and search for ideas.

My WOW factor is silence. I step to center stage and stand in silence. I look around the audience and then glance at my watch. After seven seconds, I say, "Seven seconds. In seven seconds your mind has made a thousand computations about me." I go on to define how the mind makes unconscious automatic decision about another person in seven seconds. At the conclusion of my WOW factor, I make a point. The point of the song, story, quote, statistic, improvisation, role play, or seven seconds must lead the audience into the talk. For example, the point of the seven-second exercise is to demonstrate how a prospective buyer makes unconscious decisions about you in nearly no time, and those impressions will make or break the success of your talk and your offer. Every WOW factor needs a point consisting of two to three quick sentences to help the audience understand what is in store for them.

Here are two more examples:

The *Cookie Thief* story is about a woman eating cookies from what she thought was her own bag, as was the man sitting next to her. She gets aggravated, only to find out that she was actually eating out of his bag. The point to the story for your audience could be how people can be quick to judge or draw conclusions without knowing the whole story. Sometimes we need to see the bigger picture and exercise forgiveness or even apologize.

The *This is Good for the King and His Servant* story is about a servant with a habit of saying, "This is good" about whatever happens, even when the king's thumb is shot off. The point of the story, depending upon the content or purpose of your talk, might be that attitude colors everything. What is your perspective? How do you see the conditions in your life, business, health, or relationships?

Multiple stories can work for your WOW factor. Be sure to make a point for every story you tell. Never tell a story without a point, and never make a point without a story. Story-telling selling is the best way to connect and close your audience. Not only does it serve them best, but it's also the most fun for everyone.

3) POSITION ME

The third step to creating a big income talk is to establish credibility, expertise, and authority. I call this step "Position Me." This section of your talk sets up your expert positioning right off the bat. When you establish your status as an expert, you command power. Now is the time to show off your accomplishments. You audience looks to you for learning. It is your job to show them that you are the expert for them. The audience will mirror your confidence and energy, so establish yourself early.

Accomplish Position Me with four or five sentences that demonstrate you are the go-to expert. Tell of your success and why you are uniquely qualified to be on this stage. You are in front of this audience for a reason. Your display of confidence and expert experiences will validate that you belong there.

Positioning might sound like this:

> I created two multi-million-dollar businesses.

> I founded two organizations that secured over four million dollars in donated funds.

> I helped people collectively lose over eight hundred pounds in six months.

> For more than twenty-five years, I have been a coach and consultant to Fortune 500 Companies like XYZ.

The point of these statements is to position yourself as the leader. The best way to find your top positioning statements is to write down every single job you have had and every problem you have solved. In your solutions, include the results you generated, such as statistics and dollar amounts.

My Position Me statement: "I am Jane M Powers, and I created two multi-million-dollar businesses and a six-figure coaching business in my first year with fewer than three hundred people on my list. Entrepreneurs hire me to speak with confidence and sell with authority from any platform to connect, capture, and close their ideal audience. I have been professionally speaking and selling for thirty years, and as a Turn-Around Specialist, I have increased profits by 240% in less than eleven months."

4) POSITION THEM

Now that you are positioned as the expert, "Position Them." To make a meaningful connection with your audience, position their pain and their problems. Bring their awareness to their top-of-mind pain, problem, or question. This vital component helps the audience see that you understand their frustration, their pain, and their problems. Authenticity is paramount—crucial to audience engagement and enrollment. A talk that sells is filled with stories and authentic sharing that causes the audience to lean in and be eager for more. They want what you have to offer because they feel connected, they trust you, and they appreciate that you get them!

Create the Position Them section by identifying your audience's pain point. The best way to determine their pain or struggle is to research before you speak. Ask the host what the group's top-of-mind struggles and problems are. You can also interview members of the group or organization. When the planner, organizer, or host books me, I ask for three or four people I can interview to get to know the audience. I also look at past speakers and events to find out who has spoken before and on what topics. It is good to know which topics were a hit and which ones bombed. I have even gone so far as to check out websites for members, industry issues, and concerns in their blog or publications. Research as much as possible to capitalize on the opportunity to relate to the audience in an informed manner. This is the best way to connect with more people and convert more sales.

Now that you understand positioning both yourself and your audience, create a smooth transition from one to the other. The best way is to tell the audience your story of struggle and triumph. Show them you relate to their problems and that you can overcome them yourself. This positions you as the expert and demonstrates that you have the answer to their pain.

To transition from Position Me to Position Them, I share my story about the crumbling of the real estate market in 2008. I tell how I was flying high, with my organization ranking in the top three percent in the state of Arizona. I was a seven-figure broker and loving every minute of it! I rode the wave of success, and then the wave fell out from under me. To further relate to the audience, I ask, "Does anyone remember what happened in 2007 and 2008?" I tell them I remember it well! The market came to a screeching halt. I went from million-dollar sales to celebrating a fourteen-thousand-dollar sale. I close with, "The good news is I slept like a baby—I woke up every two hours and cried!" The audience loves the humor. They relate to what happened in 2008, and they know that I understand what it means to struggle.

Next, I Position Them by making this point: "Some of you may be sleeping like a baby, and some maybe not sleeping at all because you are not converting your audience, your business is stagnant, and you are frustrated." That relates my story to their pain. Love it?

Here are more samples to transition your positioning statements:

Sample 1: I wasn't always in the top three percent of my industry. I learned the hard way the three biggest challenges costing entrepreneurs thousands of dollars and months of time. One is having a purpose with no plan. Two is operating in to-do overload. And three is working way too hard for way too little. Are you feeling those challenges? If so, you are probably feeling frustrated, and that blocks the stream of high paying clients from entering your pipeline.

Sample 2: I wish I could say I kept more money than I spent my first year or two in business, but that is just not true. I was not making enough money, I lacked clarity, and my message was not selling. Some of you might be in the same boat.

Sample 3: My current list of ten thousand sounds impressive compared to my early list that was all of three hundred. Like so many entrepreneurs, I did not stand out. My lists were too small, my niche was too broad, and the learning curve was too high. Some of you are experiencing just that, and you are living through too many ups and downs. The stress and inconsistency, not to mention high expenses with low returns, are way too much. I get it. You can get stuck, and what I know is that *stuck stinks*! I am all too familiar with stuck. Being familiar with stuck is bad enough. What's worse is being stuck and not even realizing it.

The purpose of the first part of your talk is to WOW your audience into engaging with you and then tapping into your expertise because you have made them profoundly aware of their own pain.

5) PROMISE

Step five of the talk is your "Promise." What will you share with them during your time together? Explain your commitment to them. Explain what they will experience and what transformation will happen as a result of your talk. This answers their problem and solves their Position Them pain. If you have successfully positioned them, your Promise will have them eagerly anticipating the rest of your talk. They will be hooked! In this segment, you will communicate precisely what solutions you provide and steps they can take to achieve results. You will state three to four objectives to help them manage their expectations. I use a simple template formula for every single talk I deliver, and I recommend you do so as well. Use this exact layout to deliver a confident solution and powerful promise:

> *Today, I am going to show you some proven and simple, yet highly effective tools that will help you speak with confidence and sell with authority so that you gain exposure, grow your list, and build your bank account. You will walk away with three key elements in your message that make you money. You will also begin to create a big-impact, big-income INTROmercial™ that will connect, capture, and close your ideal clients. You will discover key steps to help you successfully sell from any platform without selling a thing.*

> *You will bust through any blocks that keep you from speaking or selling so you can generate real results with a big impact and big income. I will give you everything I possibly can in the time allotted. I will also give you an opportunity to connect with me for additional resources. Fair enough?"*

This promise is straightforward and addresses their pain, which you stated in the Position Them section. The final statement of your promise, *I will also give you an opportunity to connect with me for additional resources,* is very important. You are saying up front that you will be inviting them to take action, meaning you will be making an offer. Not only does this help you be authentic, it also keeps your promise to provide them a resource. Believe it or not, many people fail to make an offer. They forget it, avoid it, or run out of time. Unfortunately, you can't sell without an invitation.

I spoke to corporations for over seventeen years and delivered training to organizations. I was paid to speak and to enroll people into more training workshops. In those days, I didn't even have a call to action. I didn't leverage my time on stage. I got a ton of hugs, but hugs don't pay the bills. I didn't know what I didn't know. I had nothing to sell.

In 2010, I transitioned into full time coaching and knew I had to have an offer. I created a program, and when the time came to sell from stage, I either ran out of time or rattled off the offer ineffectively. I counted on my follow-up efforts to make the offer and close the deal. Luckily, I am really good at follow-up and sales. Otherwise, I would have been in real trouble.

You *must* make an offer, whether it is free or paid. It is your responsibility to give the audience a means by which they can grow and succeed. Your Promise informs the audience that you will give them a resource to solve their problem, and that is your call to action. The Promise will vary depending on the audience and what you want to provide them.

You now know where to begin, how to position yourself and your audience, and what you want to provide them. The next step is to provide it through rich, informative, meaningful, and robust content.

6) PROVIDE CONTENT

Ralph Waldo Emerson said, "Speech is power: speech is to persuade, to convert, to compel." The content of your talk is to do exactly that: persuade them to align with your view, convert them into buyers, and compel them to act. This is accomplished with your expert subject matter. Your content is a summary of the basic teachings of your work in the world. My expert content is about sales, whether you are speaking, networking, or selling a product. I am a sales expert, and with my content I deliver my most compelling information and strategies for people to create greater success. What is your expert subject matter? What do you believe your ideal client needs to know?

Make your content a precise balance of statistics, stories, and facts. The ratio is vital to the success and delivery of your talk. With too many stories, you get lots of hugs (which don't pay the bills). With too many facts, the audience doesn't get to know you (you don't form a trusted relationship). With too many statistics, you risk losing a huge percentage of your audience to boredom and catnapping. An audience will forgive you for just about anything except being boring and ordinary.

Keep a story journal with ideas to weave into your content. I always keep my journal with me, and when I remember something that happened to me, I put it in my journal. Your journal will be a good source for stories to connect you with your audience. In your stories, maintain the right I:You ratio, with more *you* references than *I* references. The audience wants to learn about themselves, not to hear you tell about you. For a balanced ratio, tell your story with *I* focus, and express the story point and the teaching with *you* focus.

I also note in my journal quotes, teachings, and concepts I encounter. These make great content for talks, blog posts, videos, and social media. Convert what you know into a formula or a three-step process to ramp up the power of your content.

Keep in mind what your audience already knows. If they know nothing or very little, create content that is basic or entry-level. This might sound obvious, but you would be surprised how many talks I evaluate that are so high level that the speaker can't understand why no one bought. Don't lose your audience with information that is over their heads. In contrast, don't deliver elementary basics to an advanced group. Know your audience and your material. Always underestimate your audience and overestimate yourself! Don't assume they know what you do, and don't minimize your brilliance.

Know your material and your talk formula. There will be times you need to change your talk on the fly. A number of years ago when I was hired to speak at a conference, I received a call from the event host. She provided the location as the Parks and Recs Building. I don't know how it happened, but I thought my audience was the Parks and Recs of Arizona and not the conference of Homeowner Association Managers, Vice Presidents, and Presidents. I arrived at the venue and realized I had made a huge mistake. The good news is I deliver essentially the same talk using the same formula. It allowed me to shift gears easily and deliver a commanding talk with rave reviews. The Speak to Profit formula is a one-size-fits-all talk. You can adjust it to speak for five minutes or five days. You can switch out the Position Them portion to meet the specific audience. Trust me, this formula frees up massive time for you to go out and sell instead of writing and re-writing your talks.

For powerful content, use a three-point structure:

1. Where are you?
2. Where do you want to be?
3. How do you get there?

Or this alternative:

1. What's wrong?
2. Why is it wrong?
3. How do we make it right?

Other ideas for content creation could be the first three steps in your seven-step system, three facts about weight loss, or the top three game changers in your business or life. They must be informative, educational, applicable, and inspirational. Make sure your material is entertaining and engaging as well as relevant and useful. Let your content provide an opportunity to be interactive and conversational.

An acronym is another system to create effective talks. I recommend limiting acronyms to three letters. For example, W.I.N., O.W.N., I.A.M., Y.O.U., F.U.N., K.E.Y., F.I.T., L.U.V., or W.H.Y. It doesn't even have to be a real word. You can make up an acronym to best deliver your content.

The only condition to creating content is that you teach what you know and love! Begin by brainstorming content and gathering ideas. Next, write it word for word as you would deliver it. Then —don't kill me—cut it in half! I am serious. I guarantee your talk will be too long. The problem with content is if you give too much, your listeners are overwhelmed and won't move into action, or they think they have enough information to do it themselves. Give them just enough to be aware of their pain and that you are the person to help them. The biggest mistake most speakers make is giving away too much information. It is truly a disservice to the audience. Offer enough to help, but not so much that you hinder.

Please do not proceed with the next section until you have created a basic outline or some content for your talk. The basic foundation of your talk is the most important part of your work and, ultimately, the rate at which you close the room. The following information is to be added after you have mastered the creation of your content and memorization of your talk. The items I am about to introduce will be strategically placed in your talk. You won't know where to put them until the talk has been created.

Once you have created your talk, you will weave in seeding, testimonials, examples, and successes to inform the audience about your work in the world. These will help you close the deal. Be genuine in your delivery, not canned.

a. **Seeding**. Seeding is the art of casually mentioning something that you offer, do, or have done in your business. This piques interest and curiosity and makes selling easier. If they are your ideal clients, the seed will trigger them to inquire about how you can help them and makes them more open to listening to you.

In fact, they might even pursue you to find out more!

b. **Services.** As you share a useful tip, piece of advice, or a teaching point, direct the audience to your website or to a good resource. Guide them into your product funnel with a freebie, a lead magnet, or other mechanism to engage them. You can also mention a service that isn't part of your offer. For example, if you are speaking to sell your base program (remember, offer only one thing!), you can still mention something that happened on one of your VIP Days, so your audience knows you offer that service, too.

c. **Shared testimonials.** A good testimonial is by far the best way to demonstrate social proof. Share testimonials casually and naturally: "Oh, that reminds me of a client I worked with . . ." Now share your wins and how you were instrumental in those wins.

d. **Live testimonials.** Live testimonials move people to action faster than anything you can say. Nothing is more persuasive than hearing a third party (who has nothing to gain) rave about the benefits they received from your product or service. It is priceless! Make sure the person giving the testimonial is predictable. Since you may not know what they will say, I recommend you calculate and plan when and how to use live testimonials.

7) CALL TO ACTION

Phew! You have almost completed your talk. Now on to Step 7, which is your Call to Action. Strategically place your Call to Action (CTA) within the content of your talk.

You determined your CTA in Step 1, and everything in your talk revolves around it, whether it is a free or paid offer. Always include a CTA; the audience needs a way to act on the ideas you have delivered. Make your CTA relevant and valuable, whether it's a freebie, a complimentary session, a gift, a template, or a series. The CTA inspires them to move, change, advance, commit, or decide. Whether it is *yes* or *no*, it is your responsibility to make them decide.

Where should you put your CTA? The best placement and delivery for your CTA is in Step 7 of the formula. It is crucial to keep these steps in the exact order, or you will not convert. Offer your CTA too soon, and it feels intrusive. If you wait too late, they may have tuned out or packed up to leave.

Craft a seamless transition to your CTA. The method I use most often introduces the CTA as a tip or takeaway action. For example, I teach about a system and structure of support. I inform the group that they need a support structure to help them implement this new technique. I then invite them to accept my Message to Money session as their first step of support. The session helps them to implement the recommended step of getting a support structure. Once you present the CTA, describe the features, benefits, and what's in it for them. Share testimonials that support your offer. This is the sales portion of your talk—sell! Here is a sample of the Message to Money session invitation, a free offer:

> *I want to help you take your first action step and get the structure and support you need. On behalf of XYZ Group, I have carved out fifteen time slots for you to take this work a step further with a "Message to Money" session. This session allows me to get inside of your business and your talk to see where you are leaving money on the table. We will look at what is working, what is not working, and how I might be able to support you further. I have* [insert success story, credentials, and testimonial here]. *This offer is on a first come, first served basis.* [Provide sign-up forms and give directions to complete them.] *I promise that the first fifteen people who sign up will secure time with me. If my calendar allows beyond that, I can place you on my waiting list for the next available spot.*

Tip: do not limit the number of sessions in your mind. The best problem to have is too many sessions. I hear people say, "I can only handle so many sessions." I encourage you to make room on your calendar and close the sale.

Give plenty of time and attention to your CTA. Your entire talk has been moving them to this very moment when they have the privilege of deciding yes or no to your CTA. Here you might run into a mindset block. Many speakers believe they are *tricking* the audience by *selling* to them, but remember, it is a disservice to your audience not to make an offer! Your ideal client needs your resources, and what you offer gives them additional support. They have the power to accept or decline. Empower them to take action through your call to action. Your CTA should include a time limit, a specific number available, and incentive to the first few action takers. Please use your authentic style for this. By nature, people love to feel special or to get a deal. It makes them feel they have won something. It serves the purpose by motivating them into action and committing to their own success.

Your CTA is a major part of your talk. It is what makes you money and gets you referrals. Make it count!

8) CLOSE

In Step 8, we bring the talk to a close. You have nailed your CTA and want to finish with a bang. Typically, in your close, you will give a basic summary of your talking points, tips, and offer. The close is a combination of leaving a lasting impression and converting the audience. Both are equally important.

You have multiple options for closing. If a crowd is lining up to sign up for your offer, close fast and powerfully. I spoke at an event and made a paid offer to a room of 150 people. I was half way through my CTA when I announced the bonus for the first twenty buyers. Fifty percent of the room roared their way back to the sign-up table. I admit that it shocked me. No one could hear me over the commotion, nor did they care at that point. They were all discussing among themselves how they were going to buy along with the rest of the crowd. At that point, I closed my talk and headed to the back of the room. I call that my *holy cow, get off the stage* close.

In the *Book End Close*, repeat the opening of your talk, restate your WOW factor, and then review the talking points. Always include the offer in the summation. Encourage them to say yes to themselves and take advantage of your offer.

In the *Challenge Close*, create a challenge that inspires them to act. For example, I have asked them to go out and book five speaking engagements using my Speaker Success Kit. This encourages them to opt-in for the gift offered.

You can also close by using a quote and tying it to your content and CTA. For example, according to Confucius, "When it is evident that the goals cannot be reached, don't adjust the goals, adjust the action steps."

My go-to-close is to tell a fun, inspirational story. I love to leave them with a laugh and a lasting impression of my ability to connect and understand my audience. Please never offer a Q-and-A session at the end of the talk. You are and have been the star of the show. When you open the floor to questions, you run the risk of being derailed by a show stopper. Someone in the audience may challenge your content or want to know how the calls will go. Those people are a buzz kill. The audience is buzzing about you; don't let anyone take that away. You can always say, "I will be at the back of the room for questions, but first get your enrollment forms turned in." Then exit the stage.

Speak to Profit is a proven formula that converts audiences time and time again. Not only is this true for me, but it will be for you too. I encourage you to take your time and create thoughtful content that supports your offer. I have closed over $38,000 after speaking to an audience of fifteen people in a noisy restaurant with a free offer. Using the Speak to Profit formula I have closed anywhere from fifty to one hundred percent of the room by receiving their opt-in for a free offer, then converting sales in excess of $105,000. Use this talk at your live events. I have closed over $325,000 using this exact formula at my three-day event. It is powerful and results driven. The talk is set up in the exact order to convert your audience. Step into your power and create a talk that sells, every time.

CHAPTER 8
DO IT AFRAID

Nelson Mandela said, "I learned that courage was not the absence of fear, but the triumph over it. The brave man is not he who does not feel afraid, but he who conquers that fear."[17] Are you ready to speak now? I have been creating talks for entrepreneurs and professionals for more than ten years. The one thing every single one of them had in common was fear! The completion of your talk has the power to eliminate about half of the fears that your audience members experience, but you can't eliminate all the fear. Fear is a common reaction to public speaking and sales. When you speak to profit, you are selling. Selling elicits fear in even the bravest of people. To fully command your power from stage and convert your ideal client, you need to release anything that gets in your way, starting with fear of either speaking or selling or both.

I get it! I have experienced my fair share of fear, but I have yet to let it stop me. Consciously or unconsciously, people give in to their fears too easily. When it's time to act, they're just not willing to take the step that creates the desired results. They feel inner self-doubt that consistently has them questioning their every move in growing their business, their income, and their life. Entrepreneurs often allow fear, worry, and doubt to dominate and define their lives. They don't even know they're being controlled by fear because the logical mind always seems to make perfect sense.

In my coaching business, I repeatedly initiate enrollment or sales conversations to invite people to work with me. During nearly every enrollment conversation, the prospect expresses her absolute, desperate desire to work with me. The expression is an emphatic, *yes,* because she knows the amount of money she can make, and she knows she needs my expertise. But about ninety percent of the time, fear kicks in when we begin to talk about the investment. People come up with every reason not to spend money. At that moment, fear drives the decision-making process. Fear makes the decision by default.

I grew up afraid each and every day of my life. I experienced abuse and the loss of my mother when I was fourteen years old. As a result, the greatest struggle in my day-to-day life, both in my business and personal life, is my dance with fear. But I continue to find ways to navigate fear and move through it while achieving continued success. You can do some simple things to feel the fear of doing nearly anything you want, and do it anyway. In *Conversations with God: An Uncommon Dialogue*, Neale Donald Walsch says, "All human actions are motivated at their deepest level by two emotions: fear or love."[18] If this is true, then it is inevitable that we will face fear and do what we can to put it into perspective, no matter if fear is of speaking, selling, or getting booked. Acknowledge that you are afraid and get to the core of it. When you express and address your fears, you will feel the charge diminishing. When you feel it, express it, and acknowledge it, fear will have less of an impact on you.

I have worked with many individuals who experience extreme anxiety when they give a presentation, talk, or sales pitch. The first thing I ask them is to give their fear a voice. I have them share what the fear is telling them, what belief or story are they hearing. Fear is simply an expression of a wound, scar, or hurt that has not healed. It is an inherited or learned story or belief, just like your money story.

I inherited my parents' money story and had a hidden fear pattern around money. I didn't realize it until I became an entrepreneur. I was always gainfully employed, and if I didn't work, I still got paid. As the owner of my own business, I knew that if I didn't work, no one would pay me. That tripped my money trigger. I began operating out of fear without knowing it. I found myself working like crazy and never feeling satisfied with the number of commas in my income. When I stopped to explore what was driving me so hard, I discovered it was fear. That was the best discovery and game-changing moment in my life. We need to understand what motivates us and what stops us. When you're stopping yourself from doing anything, you may need to express some fear.

The more you focus on fear, the more it expands and the louder it gets. Fearful thoughts attract more fear. Don't fight the fear by arguing with it; instead, drown it out with what you would love or what might be a better feeling thought. During the summer in Phoenix, Arizona, the inside of a car can feel like eight thousand degrees. But when I get into the car on a blistering summer day, I can't take handfuls of heat and throw it out the window. Instead, I crank up the air conditioning and wait for it to overtake the heat.

That's exactly the way to deal with fear. Turn up the volume on what you would love, and your positive thoughts will attract more of the same. Instead of expecting the worst, train your mind to expect the best. Make positive assumptions about your actions and overtake your fears. Don't give time, attention, or energy to fear.

Aristotle spoke of fear as the opposite of confidence. To him, the world was reducible to pairs of opposites, (hot and cold, wet and dry). Great men and women have overcome fear's effects. Their cure for fear was to act in virtuous ways, including being courageous. Much in contrast to today's mantras, Aristotle did not advocate the pursuit of fearlessness. To be fearless was a sign of imbalance. It was considered crazy not to fear the gods and the all-consuming influence they had on the environment.[19]

Most of us try to achieve fearlessness by doing everything we can to get rid of the fear. The problem is we are working against our own ego. As John O'Donohue, author of *Anam Cara: A Book of Celtic Wisdom*, says, "The ego is the false self—born out of fear and defensiveness."[20]

The ego's self-appointed function is to help you get what you think you need from the world and prevent you from losing what you have. It's fueled by fear and sees threats everywhere. This fear leads inevitably to feelings of separation, lack, competition, judgment, grasping, and deep loneliness—in other words, suffering. The ego creates fear to keep us safe. Our ego wants to avoid at all costs rejection, overwhelm, humiliation, mistakes, complete loss, the unknown, and anything else that appears to jeopardize the status quo. We all experience fear. What separates those who are successful and those who allow fear to hold them back is the willingness to move forward and do it afraid.

The best way to move through fear is to face it as a companion and not as an enemy. Fear serves us by showing us where we need to heal or work on our confidence, faith, and belief. It takes courage and effort to face our fear. The more we do it, the more we prove to ourselves that we are fully capable. We do not have to eliminate fear. Simply acknowledge it and take action afraid. Move outside of your comfort zone. People tend to avoid discomfort at all costs. They smile, talk, or procrastinate to avoid moving outside their comfort zone. But success comes when we learn to be comfortable in the discomfort. Are you willing? Are you willing to trade short-term discomfort for long-term success?

Surely you remember what happened in 2008 with our economy. I was an extremely successful real estate broker and suffered a tragic adjustment in my income. To say the least, I was thrown outside my comfort zone. I had always been successful in my business. The market crash forced me to market, sell, and operate my real estate business in an entirely new way. I knew that I would feel very uncomfortable in creating a new business. I knew if I could put some systems in place—feeling fear and doing it anyway—I would reestablish my success in real estate. To experience long-term gain, I suffered short-term discomfort. I had many days filled with tears and frustration. Are you willing to do what you haven't done? Are you willing to move beyond your comfort zone?

Bob Proctor says, "There is a single mental move you can make which, in a millisecond, will solve enormous problems for you. It has the potential to improve almost any personal or business situation you will ever encounter . . . and it could literally propel you down the path to incredible success. We have a name for this magic mental activity . . . it is called DECISION."[21] The power of decision helps us navigate fears and act quickly and with confidence. We build confidence by taking risks and making decisions. Risk requires courage, which feeds our confidence. Confidence minimizes fear. Taking decisive action is instrumental in successfully befriending fear. Time and time again our inner self-doubt makes us question our decisions and keep us from acting. Opportunities are offered to us every day. If we do not act on them, we will stay in our comfort zone or status quo.

Reevaluating perspective about success starts with making a decision. Once we decide to succeed, it's time to commit to whatever it takes to make it so. It comes down to taking bold and decisive action toward what we say we want. It's saying yes to what's possible, saying yes to the opportunities we are given, and then taking decisive action.

You have made numerous decisions in your life and career, some good, some bad. A great way to move into action and through your fear is to shift perspective. What success have you achieved? We often discount our success because we are too busy focusing on what we haven't yet achieved. We will never be happy with our *now success* if we compare it to our *vision* of success. I have worked with people who make six figures and are not satisfied because they are not making seven figures. And there are people who are unhappy about losing ten pounds because they want to lose twenty pounds.

To strengthen our belief in ourselves, we need to recognize and appreciate every success along the way. Discover what you can celebrate by writing down every paid or volunteer job you have had and every problem you solved in those positions. You will discover skills, talents, and extraordinary accomplishments you never realized you had. Remember when I told you I did this activity and discovered that in one position I held, I increased profits by two hundred forty percent in eleven months? I have to say, it increased my confidence by two hundred forty percent! What have you done that you need to celebrate?

Celebrate with people who share your outlook, vision, and desire for success. Surround yourself with successful people who can naturally hold the same belief for you. Robert Fulghum said it best in his book, *All I Really Need to Know I Learned in Kindergarten*: "When you go out into the world, it is best to hold hands and stick together."[22] Sticking together makes tough times easier and easier times more fun! No one can do everything alone. When left to our own supervision, most of us will drive ourselves crazy. We need a support structure that helps us remember who we are and what we bring to the world. Select your support system carefully. We encounter people each day who live according to their own version of fear. Surround yourself with people who think from possibility and who believe in you.

CHAPTER 9

TIPS AND TRICKS FOR PROFITABLE SPEAKING

Like I have said, I love speaking, and in more than thirty years of stage time, I have discovered a number of tips and tricks to ensure a command performance. The Speak to Profit formula will eliminate half of your fears. Now, let's work on the other half. Mastering your delivery is an ongoing process. Every presentation you deliver will improve as you gain experience from the platform.

In my live-stage experience, I mastered the art of delivering a compelling talk that sells. Then I was introduced to technology—specifically, video. Great live speakers are not necessarily great at speaking on video. From stage, I was vibrant, vivacious, entertaining, and personable. It turns out video was not my best art form. I made a number of dreadful videos that I could barely bring myself to watch. It was not until someone wanted to charge me $3,500 for a three-minute video that I decided to get over my fear and record. I took all my stage tips and tricks and transferred them to my video performance. The following are tools you can use on and off stage to capture and close your ideal client.

Let's start with the most basic speaking tip, picking the right time of day to speak. The best time to present is in the morning after ten o'clock. You may be asked to speak during meals, happy hours, and the ever-popular just after lunch. Be prepared! Do not try to talk over the servers or pretend it isn't distracting. I like to *paint it red* or point out the obvious. I will stop and help the server or comment on their great service. I make everyone a part of the talk, because they are! My favorite ploy is to point at my table and threaten the crowd within an inch of their lives if they eat my dessert. Bring your audience into your talk and build the connection by being real.

Speaking at the right time is important, but it's even more important to end on time. Never go over the allotted time! Always abide by the schedule, or I guarantee you will not be invited back or referred. Rehearse your talk with a timer. You will know how much time you have to speak beforehand, so structure your talk accordingly. Be prepared. I was invited to speak at a real estate event for a one-hour-and-fifteen-minute time slot. The gentleman before me went rogue and literally would not be removed from the platform. He went thirty minutes into my time. As a result, I was forced to adjust my talk and nail the close in almost half the time. That's not the only time this has happened to me, and I guarantee it will happen to you if you are out there speaking in the world. The good news is that the formula allows you to take out a section as necessary. If you need to adjust your talk, start by reducing the content. The best approach is to present the highlights of your three teaching points. Another option is to deliver only one of the points. Paring down your talk is easy with the formula. Just be sure you follow it in the exact order recommended.

No matter the length of the talk, it's critical to make an emotional connection with the audience, on or offline. Connection is key to a successful presentation. Connect with the audience by engaging them. Ask questions, implement activities, do share-with-your-neighbor exercises, make them stand up, sit down, think, imagine, do, and more. Get them involved. Don't let them sit there and listen to you the entire time, unless you are entertaining and on a roll. People will forgive you for just about anything but being boring. Stay awake and engaged. Make them think and participate by asking *how many?* or *who?* This allows the audience to share about themselves with you and the other participants. *How many* is a survey question. It's a survey that gives you an idea of the room's experience. *Who* reveals the audience's desire and creates buy-in. The closer you get to the offer, the more *who* questions you ask. It connects you with the audience, and with that interaction, you gain trust.

I love interacting with the audience to build trust and bring the focus of the room together. I ask someone in the front of the room to please keep me on track. I have memorized my talk formula; therefore, I have the freedom to go off on tangents and know exactly where to re-start my talk. But on occasion I get so involved in my tangent that I'm not sure where I left off. So, I turn to my person and ask them where the heck I was going with that. The audience loves it, and the chosen person has yet to fail me. They recite exactly what I was saying. Choose a person one who is taking notes or looks attentive and ready to go. Another way I interact is to ask volunteers to demonstrate my *parlor trick*. A parlor trick is a skill or talent you have that wows the audience. Mine is to create an INTROmercial™ on the spot in a matter of minutes. I have also been known to *code* a person's selling style in seconds.

My events booth banner displays one of my parlor tricks: "Give me 20 seconds and I will find $20,000 in your business." I *can*! People will volunteer their time for twenty seconds. I simply ask them what their work is in the world. In under twenty seconds, I stop them and tell them exactly where they are losing money. One of my clients is an image consultant who uses color swatches and scarves to demonstrate an individual's "season." What is your parlor trick?

Some speakers depend on too many visual aids, when a simple parlor trick is more effective. Be careful of Death by PowerPoint—a saying in the speaking industry that defines speakers who can't function without a PowerPoint presentation. My rule is no PowerPoint (PP) if your talk is shorter than sixty minutes. And if you do use PP, don't talk too much. Let the PP do the work. Nothing is more insulting than a presenter who reads the PP line by line. I once attended an event where the speaker literally had her back to the audience the entire time as she read the screens to us. I gave her some leeway because she was new to presenting, but the best result from PP comes by using only a few words and letting your PP pictures inspire the minds of the audience. I use no more than six to ten words per slide. Pictures engage the right hemisphere of the brain and help people enjoy your presentation more. Some audience members will want a chart, graph, or statistic, so make sure you include at least one image to keep them engaged. Props are also fun and engaging, but don't overdo it.

Too many PP slides can cause audience overload. They become overwhelmed and shut down. If you give away the kitchen sink during your talk, you lose audience engagement. Too much information will have a negative effect on your sales results.

Use a variety of activities, exercises, call-backs, parlor tricks, and interactions to engage the audience. My top tip: incorporate into every talk the exchange of power. Transfer the audience's attention from the previous speaker or host to you. That's easy if the previous speaker was boring, not so easy if they were amazing.

At the 2014 MPI EduCON (Meeting Planners International Education Conference), I had the pleasure of following a wonderful speaker, Janice Hurley. Janice is the Image Expert who works with executives and companies who want a compelling presence for optimal impact through improved visual, verbal, and body language skills. Janice dazzled the audience with her color matching and scarf and tie placements on the audience members. They simply loved her and her information. I loved her and hated her at the same time. She was a tough act to follow.

Up to that point in my career, I had never considered a makeover. I had dressed to hide love handles and sweat. I am pretty sure my outfit matched, but by no means was I a fashion standout compared to Janice. I was an amateur. I knew that I not only had to take over the stage, but I also had to distract the audience from doing a once-over on my outfit. Taking over the stage from a previous performer takes some creativity and thinking fast on your feet.

The emcee introduced me, and I stood dead center of the stage, crossed my arms, expressed irritation on my face and said, "Who in the world put together the speaking line-up?" I then pointed at Janice and simply looked myself up and down. The entire crowd knew exactly what I was talking about and felt my pain. They laughed and appeared to admire my transparency. They were mine from that point on.

When you take over the stage, either edify the previous speaker or distract the audience's focus. Another way to take over the stage is, after the emcee introduces you, lean in and say something to them. This aligns you with the person and transfers their power to you. Once you have the stage, own it. Never let your audience see you sweat, and never confess that you are nervous, tired, forgetful or anything else that will shake their trust in you. Trust your expertise, and don't undermine your credibility with qualifiers like *I think*, *I believe*, or *I feel*, unless you are actually talking about thoughts, beliefs, or feelings. The audience is in your hands, and it is your job to command authority. Open with a WOW, close with a bang, and if you are going to bomb, do it in the middle. It is critical to memorize your talk so that you can win them over and close the deal.

Engaging the audience is a must. Knowing how to read the audience is helpful. A trick to reading the audience is that *their feet don't lie*. Check the audience's feet to determine if they are still with you. If their feet are pointing at you, they are interested. If their feet point away or toward the exit, you have lost them. It is your job to reengage them and capture their interest. The best way is to tell a story. Bring them back by invoking their imagination and be sure the point of the story relates to them. A great way to keep them from heading out the door, feet and all, is to avoid sameness. Sameness is the enemy of speaking. If you follow the same cadence, vocal rhythm, pitch, tone, and gesture patterns throughout your presentation, your audience will tune you out. When you speak, be happy to be there.

I was booked to speak toward the end of the Calvary Recovery Center Managers Conference during the hot summer in Arizona. The group had been there for four days enduring budget, planning, and staffing meetings. They were spent by the time three o'clock Friday rolled around. The room was hot from the blazing sun and 115-degree temperatures. I was not thrilled to be there after climbing stairs and searching for the meeting room. Once introduced, I gave it my all. I am happy to report only one man fell asleep—that was a first in my entire career! I did everything to spice up the environment, yet I lost one to zzzzz's. The rest of the audience loved it. It was a great lesson for me. No matter how many times you give your talk, it is the first time for your audience. So, deliver it as if it's your first. Always leave them smiling. It is your responsibility to leave your audience feeling better than when they walked in.

Everything you do on stage or from any platform affects your results. People ask me what to do with their hands. I say pretend you're holding a volleyball. This looks natural and poised and provides a balance of warmth and strength for your audience. Fidgeting with your hands detracts from your overall message. Be aware that certain gestures can keep you from communicating warmth and trustworthiness—leaning away, crossing your arms, rubbing or grasping your hands together, and touching your neck, face, or stomach. To varying degrees, these motions demonstrate anxiety, self-protection, and avoidance.

Here are some other speaking tips and tricks:

STAGE PRESENCE

Movement on stage. Walking towards the audience demonstrates warmth, encouragement, persuasion, buy-in, and selling. Avoid too much lower body animation or excessive movement, as it communicates that you are unsure. Never cross your legs! It screams insecurity, and the audience will feel that you are off-balance. Upper body animation exudes authority. Staying planted says you mean what you say.

Nervous mannerisms. Shift of body weight, ringing of hands, tugging at clothes, adjusting glasses, playing with jewelry, or hands in your pockets communicates insecurity and nervousness.

Holding objects in front of your body. Notecards, notebook, remote control, even a podium indicates shyness and resistance, as if you're hiding behind the objects in an effort to separate yourself from others. Instead, carry objects at your side whenever possible.

Narrowing your eyes. If you want to give someone the impression that you don't like them (or their ideas), narrow your eyes while looking at them. It makes you scowl. A slight narrowing of the eyes is an instinctual, universal expression of anger across various species in the animal kingdom (think about the angry expressions of tigers, dogs, etc.). Some people make the mistake of narrowing their eyes during a presentation as a reflex of thinking. Don't send people the wrong message.

Looking away while speaking. Lack of eye contact with the audience indicates low interest and disengagement. Sometimes it's even interpreted as a casual sign of arrogance. Always look straight ahead and make eye contact with as many people in the audience as possible. If you are on a stage with bright lights, imagine you are able to see the entire room and scan the seats. If you are on video, podcast, or television, imagine that your ideal client is sitting behind the camera lens.

Touching your face. Face touching, especially on the nose, is commonly interpreted as an indication of deception. Also, covering the mouth is a common gesture people make when they're lying. Keep your hands away from your face when you speak.

Faking a smile. A fake smile is a sign of deception commonly seen on the face of a fraud. A genuine smile wrinkles the corners of the eyes and changes the expression of the entire face. Don't force yourself to smile, as that usually indicates you are nervous. The best way to relieve nervousness is to ask the audience a question. Turn the attention to someone or something else.

Crossing your arms. Crossed arms are a sign of defensive resistance. Some people interpret it as egotism. Keep your arms open and at your sides, unless you are making a stance. I occasionally cross my arms while listening or contemplating. I am never misinterpreted as defensive; quite the contrary. I am engaged and listening intently. Be mindful if you cross your arms or hands.

Posture. Posture is an immediate telltale sign of your confidence and composure. Your stance literally makes a stand for you, delivering a clear message about how you will be treated. It makes a huge difference in the way your audience responds to you. Place your feet a comfortable distance apart, keep your shoulders pulled back, keep your head up, and command the stage. Slouched shoulders indicate low self-esteem. People associate perked-up shoulders with strong self-confidence. Always pull your shoulders back. Not only will you look more confident, you'll feel more confident as well.

Men (and women!) keep your hands out of your pockets. This tip speaks for itself. I've seen speakers playing with loose change in their pockets. Yikes! People who feel nervous or unsure of themselves may unconsciously take a guarded stance and adopt a posture that guards one of their most vulnerable areas, their genitals. This stance pushes the shoulders forward and makes the entire body look smaller and weaker. It almost guarantees loss of respect before you even have the chance to speak a single word. Remember, keep your hands holding the volleyball and keep your shoulders back.

Be culturally sensitive. Know your audience; in some cultures, pointing is offensive. Pointing at any audience can be seen as a gesture of dominance. I happen to point at my audience often, but I don't do it until I have gained the proper amount of credibility and authority. If you are going to point, make sure you are clearly reading the audience's respect and admiration for you.

Gesture guidelines. Highlight or magnify key concepts with small, medium, and large gestures. For small gestures, use only your fingers; for medium gestures, only hinge at wrist; for large gestures, hinge at the elbow, leaving room for the extra-large gestures that originate from the shoulders, up and down. The bigger audience, the bigger the gestures. More about gestures:

- Open-handed gestures build trust and show you have nothing to hide.
- Avoid crossing midline of body. It creates a defensive wall.
- Avoid pointing. It can be threatening or accusatory.

Keep in mind that these are great tips and tricks, *not* steadfast rules. The key to being a World Class Speaker is to be *you*! The more experience you acquire, the better you get and the more naturally you will deliver your talks. Anything can happen from the platform. You have to think fast on your feet and be human.

I spoke at an event to an audience of about two hundred people. I stood backstage waiting for my official, powerful, music-filled, introduction. For that event, I had purchased my first pair of Spanx to hold everything in place, if you know what I mean. This was my virgin Spanx experience. The music blared, the crowd roared, and my introduction began. I made my big entrance through the curtain and headed for stage. At that exact moment, my brand new Spanx rolled in a single motion, landing in the crease of my tummy. It felt like the snap of a window shade. You can imagine the thoughts running through my mind. I had a decision to make the second my Spanx played that awful trick on me: do I confess what just happened or must the show simply go on? I buttoned up my jacket and didn't skip a beat. I knew I had a limited time to speak and sell, so that's what I did. When you have Spanx snapping or a change of agenda, no matter the situation, always be professional, deliver your best material, and be your best you.

PART 3

PLAY FULL OUT

CHAPTER 10

CRAFT YOUR INTROMERCIAL™

W hat if it takes only seven seconds to make or break your success? I don't know about you, but to me that feels pretty grim. Given those odds, would you love to know how to make a huge impact with a concise, compelling, and intriguing intro that sells? Would you love to feel excited when someone asks you what you do?

Believe it or not, how you answer the *what do you do* question has a dramatic impact on your business. In fact, what you tell people about what you do could be the number one stumbling block in your ability to build a business. But answer it well, and you can build the business of your dreams by getting a new prospect, customer, business partner, or advocate with greater ease. If your answer is confusing, boring, and inconsistent, you will immediately lose the other person's interest. For people to lean in and listen requires that what you share be concise, compelling, and intriguing. You have got to capture the listener's attention and make them sit up and take notice.

Your elevator pitch, or what I've coined your INTROmercial™, is one of the most important marketing tools in your tool kit. Having a well-crafted and rehearsed message will improve your success and your bottom line dramatically. Do not underestimate the power of your INTROmercial™. Let me show you how, in just seven seconds, you can have a powerful impact on your listener. I'm going to show you why your INTROmercial™ is so important, how to craft one, and how you can implement it right away. Use my handy template to create your own INTROmercial™ to connect with potential customers and business partners.

CAPTURE PEOPLE'S INTEREST

The late Chet Holmes, a master of marketing and author of The Ultimate Sales Machine: Turbocharge Your Business with Relentless Focus on 12 Key Strategies, created the "Buyer's Pyramid." According to his pyramid, at any given time only three percent of people in any market are in "buying mode." [23] Beyond that, seven percent are open to buying, thirty percent are interested but are not thinking about it, another thirty percent don't think they are interested, and the final thirty percent of people know they are not interested. These numbers represent a buying pyramid that shows what percentage of people are actively ready to buy right now. Only three percent are actively searching with the intent to make a purchase. However, there's a whopping sixty-seven percent who could be convinced to buy if you take the right approach with them.

Holmes identified these percentages to explain to business owners and entrepreneurs that their marketing efforts need to appeal to a greater audience, not just the three percent who are ready to buy. Unfortunately, most businesses only craft their marketing to appeal to the ready-to-buy three percent, alienating everyone else. This is significant for your INTROmercial™ because it means that your message needs to appeal to the entire seventy percent of people who could potentially buy from you.

If you communicate only with the intent to sell every time you connect, you will put off most of the people you speak to because only three percent want to hear your offer. If what you say is not interesting to the remaining sixty-seven percent, those people won't care, and they will probably forget about you as soon as the conversation is over. Then, when they are ready to buy sometime down the road, they will have forgotten about you. They will buy from the person who made contact with them most recently. However, when you get your INTROmercial™ right, it will intrigue buyers and potential buyers alike. Guaranteed, they'll all want to know more, AND they'll remember you when they're ready to take action!

HONE YOUR MESSAGE

To be noticed, you must deliver an impactful and intriguing INTROmercial™ or elevator pitch in a way that it is uniquely your own. Remember, you have only seven seconds to create interest and captivate the listener. Impossible? It may feel like it, but my Ultimate Impact formula is a very specific technique to craft the perfect, impactful INTROmercial™. With my formula you will get seen, get heard, and get sales, making every seven seconds count. When you apply this simple formula, you will not only capture and connect with your listener, but you'll also close them, time and time again.

Your INTROmercial™ is designed to explain your business (your expertise, products, and services) to anyone who asks what you do. Use it every time you are in front of an audience, no matter if it is an audience of one or one thousand. Include your INTROmercial™ in the Position Me section of your talk. Use this pitch at networking events and other opportunities where you get to introduce yourself. Use your INTROmercial™ every time, even if the participants have heard it before. You will begin to gain a reputation, and people will definitely know what to do and how to support you in your business. The goal is to create an impact with the opening of your INTROmercial™ in just seven seconds and finish with the remainder of the statement, totaling 17.5 seconds. We've got some work to do, so let's get started.

HOW TO BUILD YOUR INTROMERCIAL™

STEP 1: IDENTIFY YOUR TARGET MARKET.

Answer the following questions:

- WHO is your ideal client?
- WHO is your intended audience?
- HOW do they refer to themselves?

It's important for your audience to know that you are talking to them. Help them know by identifying them right up front. I begin by saying "Entrepreneurs hire me to . . . ." With that opener, every entrepreneur will lean in to listen. Why? Because they know that I'm talking about them, and people naturally listen when it's about them. Identify specifically who you are working with: women, men, coaches, authors, top producers, high-achieving women/men, corporations, groups, executives, or others. It is important to call out your ideal client. The best part about the INTROmercial™ is you can customize it to identify the specific group you are addressing. For example, if you're at a women's meeting, you can start by saying, "Women hire me." Of course, only say that if you do work with women. As a Spiritual Life Coach, I worked with a vast majority of the population. I had a niche topic, not a niche demographic. I would begin my INTROmercial™ by filling in the blank of whoever hired me, depending upon the group. I also speak and work with authors, sales executives and representatives, coaches, organizations, corporations, speakers, authors, and more. I would fill in the blank to fit the audience. For example, when I spoke to a real estate organization, I started my INTROmercial™ with, "Realtors and brokers hire me." Narrow the audience and fill in the blank to connect with your ideal clients.

STEP 2: IDENTIFY THE HOLY GRAIL THAT YOU OFFER YOUR CLIENTS.

Answer the following questions:

- What is the top benefit you provide your clients?
- What is the "I can't live without it" benefit?
- What will turn heads and capture interest?
- What's your expertise or your superpower?

Be delighted and proud to share what you do with the world. Your passion will be infectious, and your audience will be excited to hear about it, especially if it promises them an outcome they desire. The Holy Grail is your INTROmercial™ WOW factor. It is the seven seconds that will make or break gaining the attention of your listener. This Holy Grail is important, and it takes time and attention to find the perfect one. I have gone through more than one. You will test the market with your Holy Grail. Here are some examples:

"Top earners and sales reps hire me to stay on top in an entirely new way."

"Leaders hire us to break through performance barriers."

"Authors hire me to ignite their authentic power and presence."

This is my personal favorite by Heidi Mount, one of my *Cinderella Story* clients: "Dentists hire me to uncover the hidden revenue in their business." This statement alone closed thousands of dollars in business for Heidi.

My original INTROmercial™ was, "Entrepreneurs hire me to unleash the world class speaker in them." I was at an eWomen Network event when a woman asked me about my work with entrepreneurs in sales. I began telling her all about my Core Code Sales Training and explained how speaking is actually one component of sales. She had no idea that the primary focus on my business is selling. So, I quickly changed my INTROmercial™ opening to, "Entrepreneurs hire me to speak with confidence and sell with authority." My new and improved Holy Grail opened far more doors because a huge percentage of the rooms wanted me to teach them how to sell. Test out different versions of your INTROmercial™ in the marketplace. It's important that you do not tell them *how* you do what you do; tell them the greatest benefit you offer. This is the toughest part of this formula, but don't worry, I will provide you some sample INTROmercial™ statements to generate ideas of your own.

STEP 3: IDENTIFY THE PAIN OR PROBLEM THAT YOU SOLVE.

Answer the following questions:

- What top-of-mind problem do you solve?
- What pain do you help your clients get rid of?

It's vital to communicate your audience's top-of-mind problems in order to connect with them and show that you understand what they are experiencing. Your INTROmercial™ will help them realize that you have the answer to their problem or challenge. Describe their pain using three quick points. For example, I relieve the pain of being boring, confusing, and inconsistent. That not only gets attention, but people self-select as I speak to them. Some actually yell out, "That's me!" Other pain points: "drowning in corporate demands and drama, pushing to get ahead, costing them consistent results and productivity"; "lacking charisma and expression to engage their ideal audience"; "spending too much time in the trenches dealing with team and organizational complexities"; or "driving a hundred miles an hour and sacrificing your entire life to make your numbers." The pain points are easy to find if you describe what your ideal client is going through. Make a list and check it twice.

STEP 4: IDENTIFY THE KEY OUTCOMES/ BENEFITS THEY GET FROM WORKING WITH YOU.

Answer these questions:

- What will they be able to do that they couldn't do before?
- What will they have that they didn't have before?
- What will they achieve once they have your solution?

People buy outcomes. That's why it's important to highlight the outcomes in your INTROmercial™. This is where you position your Promise. The secret is to make your promises clear and concise, so that people can easily remember them when they are ready to buy. By the way, the Promise is the *benefit* and not the *features* of what you have to offer. The *how to* conversation comes later. For now, stick to what's in it for them. The best outcome is a believable, tangible result or benefit. I am not a fan of promises for an outcome of "10 X-ing your business." I have yet to see anyone who has made that promise pull it off. It is common in my market to hear promises like, "make six figures in ninety days." Your promise must be a proven outcome that you can support and stand behind. Hype doesn't sell—authenticity does.

STEP 5: CRAFT YOUR INTROMERCIAL™.

To put all the steps together and help you craft your INTROmercial™, use my Ultimate Impact formula. Let's start with my INTROmercial™ as an example: "Entrepreneurs hire me to speak with confidence and sell with authority, because most, unfortunately, don't realize they are boring, confusing, and inconsistent—and I am the only one who will tell them. So, I help them connect, capture, and close their ideal clients and stop leaving money on the table. Bottom line, every time you open your mouth you make money."

Now I'll unpack my INTROmercial™ for you into the four components of the formula:

1. **WHO** is my ideal client? *Entrepreneurs.*
2. What is the **HOLY GRAIL** I offer? *To speak with confidence and sell with authority.*
3. What **PAIN OR PROBLEM** do I help them get rid of? *Because most, unfortunately don't realize they are boring, confusing and inconsistent—and I am the only one who will tell them.*
4. What **OUTCOMES/BENEFITS** will they get when they work with me? *So, I help them connect, capture, and close their ideal clients and stop leaving money on the table.*

Optional **BOTTOM LINE** statement. *Bottom line, every time you open your mouth you make money.* Provide a bottom line that gives them a final, direct, to-the-point description of your service.

Here are examples of great INTROmercials™:

Dentists hire me to uncover the hidden revenue in their business, because most are sitting on a gold mine and don't even know it. So, I help dental practices find an extra five hundred dollars a day and get their best ROI, bring in new patients, and capitalize on the team approach to the Revenue Contribution Model. Bottom line, I help increase the level of service and money coming in.

Authors hire me to become #1 bestsellers, because most have no idea what tools and techniques they need to achieve this notable accomplishment. So, I help them gain exposure, establish expertise, and then keep their books out of the cobwebs of cyberspace. Bottom line, they attract their ideal clients and treat their book as their business.

Leaders hire us to break through performance barriers and build a solid performing team, because most are stuck in "the way it has always been done" and get the same result with a lack of true satisfaction or real results. So, we help them deconstruct the myths of red tape, budgets, and old operating systems. Bottom line, we help remove organizational limitations and fears using our Strength Based System that creates high performing teams and an organization of excellence.

Entrepreneurs hire me to help them stand out in the marketplace and attract a steady stream of ideal clients, because most are selling to everyone and anyone, therefore, selling to no one. So, I help them showcase their genius and fill their sales funnel to create a steady stream of cash. Bottom line, I help them make more money doing what they love.

Successful Business Women/Entrepreneurs hire me to be the authority in their space, because most are invisible with no online presence, exposure, or visibility. So, I help them using my FBLive Ninja secrets to gain camera confidence, jump into the spotlight, and attract a flood of ideal clients. Bottomline, if clients aren't throwing credit cards at you, you need to get the credibility and visibility you deserve.

Growth-minded business owners hire me to disrupt their hit-or-miss, inconsistent marketing and rescue their online reputation. Most are intimidated by digital marketing and avoid technology, so I help them execute a consistent, powerful, digital presence that delivers ROI every time.

Women hire me to get naked, because most are hiding behind their image and societal expectations. So, I help them tell the bold, naked truth so they can strip away doubts, fears, limitations, and have the courage to own who they are, no matter what. (By the way, her book is The Naked Truth: A Woman's Journey to Self-Love.)

Women hire me to break down their ever-demanding world into the simplest blueprint of success because most are living a treadmill lifestyle, drained, and dreading the day of to-do's. So, I help them stop the madness and gain a new perspective to command their surroundings and create an environment and a life that thrives.

Cancer patients and survivors hire me to get back to doing the things they love TODAY, not SOMEDAY, because most feel scared, unclear about what to do next, and in fear of a relapse lingering in the back of their mind. So, I help them befriend and navigate their cancer journey, eliminate their fears, and reclaim their power. Bottom line, they heal better, faster, and live for NOW.

Entrepreneurs and sales teams hire me to codify their message, because most are communicating ineffectively and losing their message in translation. So, I help them articulate, communicate, and accelerate their sales conversions. Bottom line, you've got to speak your buyer's language in order to convert.

INTROMERCIAL™ TIPS

Just as with your Speak to Profit formula talk, follow this exact order for the content of your INTROmercial™. The key words *hire me, because,* and *so, I help,* in that order are vital to delivering your pitch successfully. These words are what I call "pattern interrupts." A pattern interrupt is a way to change a person's state or focus. Milton Erikson, an American psychiatrist and psychologist specializing in medical hypnosis and family therapy, used the handshake induction as a formal pattern interrupt. It works like this. Say you're at an event and the speaker is going on and on. You have not heard a word he or she said. You are off on the beach somewhere in Hawaii enjoying the sun and ocean with a little umbrella in your drink. You've checked out! The words, *hire me, because,* and *so, I help* are pattern interrupt words that trigger the brain to pay attention and keep the listener from checking out.

In my INTROmercials™, I change my tone and body position each time I use one of the pattern interrupt words. The audience not only hears a different tone and stays focused, but they are visually stimulated to pay attention. A pattern can be interrupted by any unexpected or sudden movement or change. It is useful to deliver your INTROmercial™ using the key words and adding humor and laughter, gestures, voice inflections, and body movements. Also, keep it short and sweet with some punchy words to get your listener's attention and make it fun!

Ultimate Impact Template to Craft Your INTROmercial™

Use this template to craft your own concise, intriguing, and compelling pitch.

_____ ,

(your ideal client)

hire me to _____

(your Holy Grail or the top benefit you offer)

because most _____ ,

(the pain they suffer or their biggest problem that you solve)

so I help them to

_____

_____

(key outcomes or benefits they get as a result of working with you. Keep it to only 2 or 3 things, short and sweet.)

Bottom line, _____

_____

_____

_____

CHAPTER 11

GET BOOKED TODAY

Speaking is a free, fast, and fun way to grow your business. It's the ideal way to get your message out and make money doing it. But how do you get yourself in front of an audience who will buy from you? You cannot succeed as the world's best-kept secret, so finding the platforms that will help you grow and make money by securing more clients is vital. Whether you want to build your business, launch a service or product, start a movement, or just communicate your message, you need to get in front of people and tell your story. That means the next big step to get your message into the world is to get booked.

Where do you go to find your ideal audience? The short answer: everywhere. Countless groups of people are meeting on any given day, at any given time, from your neighborhood to every corner of the globe. Your job is to find them. Whether you speak for free or for a fee, you've got to know where to go that your ideal clients will see you. As a new speaker, this means you say yes to every gig and get referred to more. Speak for the sake of speaking! Remember, if you're not getting in front of people to deliver your message, then you are making it way too hard!

The fastest path to lasting cash is to speak and sell. Too many people work endless hours trying to get booked and with very little success. I have made a science of getting booked, getting referred, and getting booked again! I'm going to help you secure booking gigs that get lasting results, grow your business, and catapult your success. Finding the venue and showing up is only the beginning. At the end of your presentation, you'll want to leave 'em wanting more! First, let's get you booked.

MY TOP PICKS FOR GETTING BOOKED

I've compiled a list of all my favorite places to build your business, boost your visibility, increase your credibility, and cultivate referrals. You'll find lots of opportunities here, but they're only attainable when you put yourself and your message directly in front of people who make things happen. Let's start with trade and professional associations.

TRADE AND PROFESSIONAL ASSOCIATIONS

No doubt you've heard there's an association for everything. If you don't believe it, look online at the National and Professional Trade Association Directory. There are over ten thousand associations and an estimated eleven million formal meetings per day in the United States, resulting in more than three billion meetings per year! Odds are you can find one or more to speak at each month. Pick associations in industries that are a natural fit for your message. Contact their leadership, event planners, and human resource departments and get booked.

American Society for Association Executives https://www.asaecenter.org/
The ASAE is a great organization for building exposure and generating referrals. It consists of the executives and professional staff of member associations. You'll also find a number of vendors in the group who can help you make connections.

National Association of Women Business Owners https://www.nawbo.org/

NAWBO is the only dues-based organization representing the interests of all women entrepreneurs across all industries. It has over five thousand members and sixty chapters across the country. It's also a one-stop resource to propel women business owners into greater economic, social, and political spheres of power worldwide.

eWomen Network https://www.ewomennetwork.com/
The eWomen Network is a membership network producing more than two thousand women's business events annually, including the largest four-day International Conference & Business Expo in North America. They provide thousands of speaking opportunities showcasing the best and brightest thought leaders and experts. As a member, you get access to important resources, influential business leaders, and game-changing ideas.

Meeting Professionals International https://www.mpiweb.org/
The MPI consists of highly influential people who plan events for both public and private groups. Many organizations look to MPI members as trusted advisors and ask them for speakers and trainers for their events. In addition to being the best audience (I love speaking at their events!), they're also the hottest referral source you can have in your database.

Wikipedia's List of Industry Trade Groups in the United States https://en.wikipedia.org/wiki/List_of_industry_trade_groups_in_the_United_States

Wikipedia's List of International Professional Associations https://en.wikipedia.org/wiki/List_of_international_professional_associations

I RECOMMEND THESE STEPS FOR GETTING BOOKED WITH AN ASSOCIATION:

Step 1: Find an association you want to book.

Step 2: Send an email to the entire board and committee members. All of them! Make it short and sweet. "Hello _____, I'm reaching out to see if you welcome outside speakers. I would love to support you and your organization's success. I will contact you soon, and I look forward to supporting your organization." Put this in your own words, but do not, under any circumstances, tell them what you talk about or how you will do it. If you do, you will minimize your chances to get on their calendars by a zillion percent. (I'm pretty sure that's a scientifically proven statistic.)

Step 3: Start at the top and contact the president. Make a personal phone call to follow up on your Step 2 email. Validate their very busy schedule. Then ask to speak at their next meeting, conference, annual meeting, etc.

Step 4: If the President doesn't book you, get a referral to the person who arranges their speakers. This could be a vice president or a planning committee member.

Step 5: Call the person you've been referred to and be a name dropper! Say, "The President, _____, told me to contact you about getting booked to speak at your next available meeting." They won't know if you are a personal reference of the president or if he/she supports the booking or not. It's awesome!

Step 6: Tailor your conversation. Start out by asking more than telling and listen for cues about what to say. For example, if they say that they need someone to speak about leadership, then marvel at the coincidence that you speak on just that subject. If they need help with communicating, let them know that it just so happens to be your area of expertise. The key is to hear what they say and stick to it. You are not going to say you talk about leadership if you sell widgets. You can talk about leadership and how your widget is instrumental in supporting leaders. Integrity is vital, so give value and bring value to the group. If you cannot find a resonating connection, they are not your ideal audience.

INTERNET SOURCES

With billions of pages, the Internet is an inexhaustible source of information. If you can't find something on the Internet, it probably doesn't exist—and even if you *can* find it on the Internet, it doesn't necessarily exist! It's easy to get lost online and lose valuable time trying to find exactly what you need. Start by going to your favorite search engine and entering your target industry along with the keywords found in your presentation. See what pops up. Check out who their customers are and connect the dots. There are an extraordinary number of affiliations in the public and private sectors. Follow the Internet breadcrumbs to make your search fast, easy, and effective. Here are my favorite online places to find speaking gigs.

CONFERENCES AND TRADE SHOWS

Industries spend millions of dollars a year on conferences to stay current and interesting. They are on a perpetual search for engaging, relevant speakers. As a result, they're a great place to book an engagement. Whether large or small, they give you the chance to share your unique expertise with an audience of peers, friends, or potential customers uniquely receptive to your message.

Lanyard.com
This is a great site for finding events and conferences around the world. It lets you search by location or topic, and even lets you see which ones your friends are going to or speaking at.

Conferize https://www.conferize.com/
This online platform connects events, people, and thought leaders from every industry across the globe through its more than fourteen thousand events, four million people, and twenty million content items. You can

easily create a profile of keywords to follow, and it even lets you schedule email communications on relevant, upcoming conferences.

LinkedIn https://www.linkedin.com/feed/
If you haven't joined LinkedIn yet, you are way behind the times. Harness the power of networking. Welcome to LinkedIn, the world's largest professional network with more than 546 million users in more than two hundred countries and territories worldwide. LinkedIn leads a diversified business bringing together the world's leading professional network. Connect with me on LinkedIn at https://www.linkedin.com/in/jane-m-powers/.

Meetup https://www.meetup.com/
What's great about this site is that it takes the power of the Internet and shrinks it down to focus on your neighborhood. As the world's largest network of local groups, Meetup.com makes it easy for anyone to organize or find a local face-to-face get-together. The site has more than twenty-two million members and over 210,000 groups, and it's growing every day.

Eventbrite https://www.eventbrite.com/
The founders of Eventbrite (which acquired Lanyrd.com) believe that gathering with others is the best way for people to learn, grow, get inspired, feel connected, get healthy, give back, and celebrate. Their technology facilitates those gatherings by helping people find and attend events that feed their interests while connecting them with others who share their passions.

SOCIAL NETWORKING SITES

Social sites such as Facebook, Instagram, FBLive, and Twitter have become vital tools for businesses to communicate and connect with existing and potential clients and customers. These sites are also great places to search for organizations and events where you might speak. A word to the wise entrepreneur, do not get caught in the vortex and spend too much time on social media. My rule of thumb is if you are not making over $75,000 per year, you should be speaking, networking, and getting out from behind your computer.

FBLive is hot! Live is the best way to interact with viewers in real time. You can field their burning questions, hear what's on their mind, and check out their Live Reactions to gauge how your material and performance are received. Connect instantly with your ideal clients and hosts for potential gigs. Use Live's creative tools like filters, themes, and effects, and easily express yourself in ways that delight your followers and make it even more fun. You will gain exposure and demonstrate your ability to speak. Friend me, like me, or hang out with me on Facebook at https://www.facebook.com/JaneMPowers.

YOUTUBE

More than one billion unique users visit YouTube each month; over six billion hours of video are watched each month; and one hundred hours of video are uploaded to YouTube every minute. If you are serious about speaking, you need to be on YouTube. The secret is to drive traffic to your channel. It will display your material and personality. Be natural, informative, and professional in your videos. Make a personality video, showcasing who you are as a person, in addition to some training videos. Demonstrate you are the go-to expert.

THE SPEAKER NEXT DOOR

You don't have to look any further than your neighborhood to find great speaking opportunities. Civic organizations, business networking groups, special interest clubs, and concerned citizens' coalitions are only a few that abound at the local level. After just a couple of successful engagements, word will spread like wildfire, and you'll be tagged as the go-to speaker, resulting in a high bottom problem—how to fit all the gigs into your calendar.

LIBRARIES

Do you know how many events your library hosts each month? More than you might think. Libraries are magnets for local and regional interest groups, and librarians are in the business of sharing information. Subscribe to library newsletters and calendars to keep abreast of what they're doing. Contact event organizers and offer to make a presentation; or approach a librarian and propose your own special event. A few calls could lead you, as a local expert or professional, to securing a speaking opportunity.

CHARITY ORGANIZATIONS

Your local nonprofits are no exception. They meet as often as any other organization, and they seek creative ways to raise funds, retain staff and volunteers, and deliver services. Offer to speak on a topic relevant to their staff, or better yet, propose a special event where you would give a presentation or a series where the attendees buy a ticket or provide an in-kind donation to help the charity. You'll not only get a chance to practice your public speaking, but as a bonus, you'll be doing some good by lending a hand to organizations that are all about positive social change.

CHAMBERS OF COMMERCE

Check out the Association of Chamber of Commerce Executives, acce.org/whatisachamber. I don't mean to be Captain Obvious, but a Chamber of Commerce is an organization of businesses seeking to further their collective interests, while advancing their community, region, state, or nation. Sometimes you must join a chamber to speak there, but if it's an active chamber, the exposure can be well worth the cost of membership.

CIVIC ORGANIZATIONS

Civic organizations like the Kiwanis, Lions Club, Rotary International, and the Elks are always on the lookout for interesting speakers for their meetings. Often comprised of community and business leaders, these groups can be natural multipliers to secure additional speaking engagements. Do not discount the referral and influential power of these groups.

LOCAL GOVERNMENT AGENCIES

All local governments are charged with looking after the public good. They schedule conferences for employees, host special events for constituents, produce public service announcements, and many even have their own cable television programming. You could be the expert in the room, the voice of reason, the hotbed of radicalism, or the breath of fresh air at any number of meetings that occur within their walls. And as a bonus, you would be actively participating in your local government.

SPECIAL INTEREST GROUPS

Don't underestimate the buying power or word-of-mouth potential of your neighbors. Small groups of them are meeting all the time in book clubs, sports leagues, crafting circles, cooking and wine-tasting groups, parenting and childcare co-ops, etc. A well-delivered presentation to any of these groups can be leveraged into a wealth of opportunities.

COLLEGES AND UNIVERSITIES

Higher education institutions are in the business of imparting information to eager students and are a natural fit for speaking engagements in a whole host of ways from classrooms to clubs, honor societies, alumni associations, and PanHellenic fraternities and sororities, just to name a few.

SENIOR CENTERS

Yogi Berra, Manager of the New York Mets, once said, "It ain't over till it's over." [24] Just because the audience at a senior center may be retired or out of the loop professionally doesn't mean that delivering a speech for them is any less rewarding than other venues. If you make a good impression, be prepared to hear from their extended families, and be ready to share your message again.

LOCAL MEDIA

Newspapers, magazines, and television and radio stations are constantly looking for content. Approach them with compelling reasons why they should feature you and your message. It can be a win for them and a win for you.

SOME OBVIOUS AND NOT-SO-OBVIOUS WAYS TO FIND SPEAKING GIGS

Remember, every chance to speak is an opportunity to sell. Be bold and go after the information you need to generate bookings. Try these:

PROFESSIONAL SPEAKERS BUREAUS

A speakers' bureau is a collection of speakers who talk about a particular subject, or a company that operates to facilitate speakers for clients who want motivational speakers, celebrity appearances, conference facilitators, or keynote speakers.

A speakers' bureau will hold a database of personalities from diverse fields such as politics, sports, business, and comedy. The speakers' bureau team initiates the introduction between speaker and client and supports both parties from the primary stages of making contact throughout the booking and logistics process. Clients that require speakers include businesses, corporations, charities, educational or public institutions. A speakers' bureau helps client and speaker negotiate a speaking fee, a payment awarded to an individual for speaking at a public event. This fee is usually set by the speaker or the speaker's agent. The speakers' bureau can deal with logistics like fees, transport, accommodation and timing, or communication between speaker and client. It is very important to research and determine the standard practices of each bureau. If you're considering joining one, keep these points in mind:

- Create your speaker portfolio, letter, one-sheet, and sizzle reel.
- Bureaus are a listing service and don't always proactively pitch their speakers.
- If you're not already well-known, you may not get booked.
- Keep track of your speaking gigs. Use referrals as often as possible.

REFERRALS

Train people to refer you. I've trained professionals for years on doing business by referral, and the results are astounding. Getting referrals is the best way to flow business. Your first step is to always ask for a referral—always! Doing business by referral can easily be a huge source of growth and income. Training your people to refer you requires a step-by-step how-to formula. The first thing that is absolutely necessary is to make the referrer fully understand what you do and be trained how to articulate that. I highly recommend you share with them your INTROmercial™. Help them deliver it to prospects they are referring. The next step to referring effectively is an in-person, email, or phone introduction. Ask the referrer to connect you directly, if possible. Do not share your pricing with others. You will lose people based on pricing alone. Don't let that happen. Make sure you train your people to share with you the prospect's information.

TESTIMONIALS

Gather raving fans! Any chance you get, ask clients to write or record testimonials on your behalf. Make sure you get a letter of recommendation from your speaking gigs. You want to be a name-dropper and become affiliated with several groups and organizations. Start growing a list of companies, organizations, and corporations so that you can use them to open doors in the future. People love it when you know people.

PRIVATE, "TOP SECRET" MEETINGS

You can't imagine how many private meetings take place behind the meeting. Keep your eyes and ears open for your chance to find a way into the inner circles that do business behind the scenes. The more you connect and network, the more of these meetings you'll learn about.

USER GROUPS

Many companies have user groups that consist of people who have purchased the same product with similar interests, goals, or concerns in mind. These groups often meet regularly in person or online to share ideas.

NAME BADGES AND ATTENDEE LISTS

Make it a point at every event you attend to note the names of your fellow attendees, where they work, and what they do. Grab a copy of the official attendee list from event organizers if one isn't already included in the handouts. Ask for contact information from everyone you think might be a good lead.

COMMITTEES

Volunteer to serve on committees for everything that could help your business. Cultivate relationships with other committee members and leaders to look for the chance to share your presentation with them and their networks.

SUMMITS AND TELECONFERENCES

Online summits abound, with topics ranging from local politics to global affairs. Look for those that match your business goals and reach out to their organizers.

HOW TO GET BOOKED

Now that you know *where* to find the speaking gigs, it's crucial that you master *how* to get booked repeatedly. There is a science to navigating the booking conversation so that you are in the driver's seat and getting on the calendar in front of your ideal audience. I've created *Fail Proof Booking Tips* that have resulted in landing numerous speaking gigs, but more importantly, have generated streams of lasting cash and steady referrals from the engagements. If you implement even one of my proven strategies, you'll open the floodgates to speaking, which naturally leads to the sales conversation. We all know what comes next: cashing in and doing it again and again.

To begin, let's identify your booking style: Exhibitionist, Adaptor, or Navigator. You may exhibit characteristics of each style to a certain degree. Use the various tips for each style to get in front of your ideal audience.

Regardless of your booking style, always deliver your INTROmercial™. Make sure it is clear, concise, and compelling. Do not be boring, confusing, and inconsistent when you open the conversation about what you do.

THE EXHIBITIONIST

An exhibitionist is a person who behaves in an extravagant way to attract attention. The exhibitionist is the star of the show, the center of attention, and the action taker. If this sounds like you, then these tips should be right up your alley. Turn on your star power, jump in, and get booked today.

Be creative. Getting booked requires your creativity. It's an art form. Be willing to get creative and embrace outside-the-box thinking. Generate ideas to reach out to your prospects and be different. I use lines that are unexpected and attention getting. I use humor to establish rapport with the contact and to create interest. For example, I will leave a message after the second or third call saying something like, "Hey, I didn't hear back from you after my last message. Did we break up and you didn't tell me? Give me a call." Humor and unexpected comments are great tools to break the ice.

Ask everyone. Ask anyone and everyone to introduce you to groups, organizations, and associations to speak. Make it a habit to demonstrate your energy and ability to captivate an audience. You will be magnetic and attractive to others in the marketplace. Tell everyone you are a speaker. You can do this indirectly by mentioning casually that, "When I was a speaker at XYZ organization . . . ." Let everyone know what you do by telling stories, relating case studies, or describing clients or prior speaking engagements. I ask directly during networking events. At the end of my talk I say, "If you're interested in having me speak to your organization or at your next event, let me know."

Be the star of your own show. Make a one- to three-minute *energetic* and personal follow-up video to a conversation or encounter. It leaves a lasting impression. Include details from your meeting or conversation. Start with something like, "Hello [be sure to greet them by name, and if it's an unusual one, practice to get it perfect]! We met at the _____ meeting, and I know you are interested in _____. I'm reaching out to see if we can connect to talk about _____." Add something fun to spice it up. I have several international clients and prospects, and in the opener for my video, I speak their language, literally. Simply go to Google Translate and learn a couple of greeting lines. For the record, I do not possess the skill of speaking anything but my native language. You can imagine the fun to be had by both you and the listener when you dip into their world. My recipients love it!

Be unique. It may be a cliché, but there is only one *you*, and it's your job to convey your uniqueness to the world. Oscar Wilde said, "Be yourself; everyone else is already taken." That could not be truer. The market is noisy, and to combat the numerous distractions out there, you must be unique. What makes you a stand out? Even when you discuss something mundane or well-known, put your own special spin on it with your delivery, word choice, or visuals. Make it scream *you*, your brand, and your expertise.

Don't play "Where's Waldo?" Be seen and be heard at every meeting you attend. Go to as many events as possible and look for ways to be invited to more. Many organizations have related groups, affiliates, vendors, and others that represent a treasure trove of opportunities for you to be visible.

Get your name in print. Write articles for trade magazines, industry newsletters, local newspapers, business publications, even your neighborhood association. You want your name to show up in as many places as possible.

Send personal invitations for your speaking events. When you book a gig, ask the organizers if you can invite some special guests to hear you speak. Then look through your database and invite the influential, connected, and master networkers. Oh, and don't forget your raving fans. They are your best source of advertising.

Get on the radio. Public speaking is, after all, an auditory medium, and what better way to build your reputation as a competent, engaging speaker than through the primary audio media out there? Tune in to your local talk radio station, learn what their programming is all about, and offer yourself as a subject matter expert or storyteller extraordinaire. Who knows? Chances are, you'll be heard by someone who becomes your number one prospect. You may book a gig right over the airwaves!

Practice, practice, practice. Especially when you're first starting out, don't turn down a gig. Every time you speak is an opportunity to get better. You want to get so good that they come looking for you.

Become social media savvy. The importance of social media today is well recognized, but—Warning!—don't spend too much time in this tangled web. It's a real time sucker! Get smart about how you search for and share information on social sites. Turn on your Laser Focus Superpower before you jump in.

Brand yourself. What do I mean by branding? Branding consists of cohesive, intentional visuals and words that are RECOGNIZABLE and UNIQUE. Consistency is the secret to effective branding, so be sure your message, title, tag line, colors, and images always reflect your individual brand. If you're just starting out, it's okay to continue to evolve and refine your brand but pick one or two things right out of the gate to stick with as you tweak the rest.

Be your best you—all the time, every time. It's trite, but true that, "You never get a second chance to make a first impression." Be at your best whenever you step out. Show the world your energetic, fun, confident self, whether you're in the parking lot or on the stage. Their first impression of you will stick with them long after you've left the building.

THE ADAPTOR

An adaptor is a person who connects people or organizations that have different but similar goals and designs that make them compatible work partners. Are you the social organizer? Are you the one who plans all your family get-togethers? Are you the one everybody calls first to find out what's happening? If so, then you're an adaptor. These tips should fit right in with your social nature and be just the ticket to booking gigs.

Train your fan base. You will attract legions of fans to your awesomeness, and it's crucial that they know exactly what you do and how to talk about you. As a natural magnet of energy and a fount of information, you need to teach people to refer you to their friends and networks. It's important, though, that you take charge of the action. Get contact information for the person or entity you are referred to, and personally follow up to close the deal.

Connect the dots. You've heard of six degrees of separation, right? Make it your new favorite game to see how many ways you can connect what you say and do with as many organizations as you can reach at any given time. Demonstrate how well you fit your audience's vision by providing a résumé and speaker's profile that relates directly to their mission and goals. Speak their language. Always connect the dots between your contacts. Ask them who is a good referral for them to align with their success. It opens the door for you to teach them how to connect your dots. Market mastery means teaching others to do your marketing for you. Enroll people to hire and refer you. Be in the forefront of their minds. You help them; they help you. It's what makes the business world go 'round.

Prove people like you. Everybody wants to know that the product they're buying or the person they're trusting has the stamp of approval from people just like them. That's why it's so important to get testimonials from people who have heard you speak. These endorsements carry even more weight when they come from well-respected people or organizations that have a positive reputation and influence in your subject area. Spread these endorsements around like sunflower seeds and watch opportunities blossom.

Bon appétit. Say it with food. If you can't personally take them out for lunch or happy hour, send a gift certificate from a fabulous restaurant, bakery, coffee shop, or pizzeria along with a personal note. My most successful *bon appétit* delivery is a table setting–complete with a placemat from the restaurant, plastic ware, napkin, and paper plate–glued in the pizzeria to-go box with a gift certificate and a note saying, "This is just a slice of what you'll get when we work together." They won't be able to say no to you.

Be genuine. Be yourself and everything will be great. Your natural gift generates rapport with prospects and customers. Closed-off people get chilly reactions from others. Approach rapport building with the intent to be genuinely warm and friendly. Smile, give a firm handshake, make eye contact, and engage.

Show interest. This may come as no surprise, but people are self-focused. That's great in sales, because you need to learn about your prospects before you can provide the best solutions. People want to feel invited to share what they're thinking, including their desires, fears, and problems. The more genuinely interested you are, the more relaxed and willing to share they're likely to be.

Don't be needy. Most of us know someone who wanted desperately to be liked. In desperation, we appear needy and conspicuous. We cannot force rapport. Show interest, but don't be subservient, overly friendly, or too pushy, or you will only be a turn-off. Needing your prospect more than they need you is not a recipe for success.

Give genuine compliments. Notice others and their surroundings. Genuine compliments are endearing. If you like someone's office, their website, or their outfit, say so. If your prospect had a recent accomplishment, relay your authentic congratulations. This goes a long way towards building rapport, and your prospect will appreciate it.

Practice active listening. There's nothing more frustrating in a conversation than a party who doesn't listen. Try some of these active-listening lines to show your contact that you're paying attention: "Tell me more about _____." "What does that mean for you/the business?" "What I hear you saying is _____." "Why is that?" "What I take away from that statement is _____." My all-time favorite information-generating statement is, "Interesting. Tell me more."

Calibrate the rapport. Judge the right amount of time for chitchat. It's easy to misread the prospect and spend too much time chatting. As a result, the prospect gets antsy to get down to business. Read the other person and feel for the right amount of rapport-focused conversation. Also read the culture. Be yourself, but at the same time, you can adjust your approach. Don't change who you are to fit the culture but be aware of how the culture works and how it best responds.

Know your contact's persona. If you know who you're talking to or you have some background information, it's easier to establish rapport. Start by getting a feel for your contact's personality or by researching subjects that interest her. Express curiosity, and remember, it is important to be you. People will relate to authenticity and genuine conversations over faking it or saying what you think they might want to hear.

Build trust. Your prospects learn to trust you when you do what you say you are going to do. Keep your commitments, call when you say you will, and always follow through. Don't make promises you can't keep. When people make well-intentioned commitments, only to find themselves unable to fulfill them, they may not always lose the sale, but they're certainly not building the kind of trust that makes that prospect anxious to give referrals.

Another way to build trust is to demonstrate your interest in their well-being beyond your own profit potential. Know and appreciate your prospect's needs beyond the sale. See what you can do to help him meet those needs. Little things like finding information for him or putting him in touch with other resources or giving him a free gift make a big impact.

THE NAVIGATOR

A navigator is someone skillful at plotting or directing a route through known or unknown terrain. Are you a walking, talking GPS? Do your friends call you when they're lost, both literally and figuratively? Do you have a knack for finding the closest parking space to the door or the fastest way around pesky road construction? If you approach life like Christopher Columbus, then you are the navigator. Hop right into these tips and find the shortcut to success.

Do your homework. Never, ever go in cold! Know your prospective audience, what they like, who they serve, their biggest challenges. Every little piece of information can tell you something important that can make a huge impact on the effectiveness of your presentation or connection. Find out who has made speeches to the group in the past and what kind of feedback they received. Stay up to speed on the latest trends in their industries, know who the biggest movers and shakers are and what the future holds. KNOW THY CUSTOMER! (Consider it a commandment.) Oh, and did I mention: never, ever go in cold!

Navigate past the gatekeepers. Whether literally or figuratively, you must find your way to the right people. NEVER capitulate to the gatekeeper's instructions to "just send us some info so we can get back to you." That is the kiss of death, and if you give in, you might as well just book your plane ticket to nowhere. When faced with those boilerplate words of gatekeepers everywhere, pull out my scientifically proven rebuttal: "I would love to send you information, but I know how busy you are, so maybe you could tell me the top two problems or complaints your group has that I can address." The key is to do enough research to know where you need to go and the most direct route to get there. NEVER fall into the "just send information" abyss.

Be your own bookie. It's wonderful to have a booking agent (aka, someone who will call on your behalf to get you gigs). It's sexy, sassy, and shows you've arrived. But I guarantee that you'll book twice as many gigs if you make the call yourself. You are the product, and people will want to take you for a test drive before they buy. Let them experience you.

Coffee works wonders. Can't get onto someone's calendar? Send them a note that reads, "I'm sorry we haven't had time to meet, but if we had, I would've brought you coffee." Enclose a Starbucks gift card with your note, or better yet, show up in person with a mug or cup. See how fast the promise of caffeine gets you in the door!

Faster than a hard-cooked egg. Here's what I call the Timer Method. Promise your contact that you'll only take two minutes of her time and use a timer—heck, use an egg timer, if they still make 'em. Set the timer. Then (and this is the most important part) stick to your two-minute limit. Be awesome in those two minutes and be sure to leave enough time to book a follow-up appointment. Remember, practice your pitch before you connect, so you can eliminate the small talk. Hone in on only what she needs to know and what she'll lose if she doesn't book you.

Lights, camera, action. Make a short video of yourself (no more than three minutes) giving a sample of what they'll get when they book you.

Close the video with the all-important what's-in-it-for-them segment and leave 'em wanting more.

Tap into your inner Magnum, P.I. Thanks to the Internet, it's easy to find out almost anything about almost anybody. Research your targets to find out their birthdays, special interests, favorite sports teams, alma mater, or any fact that you can acknowledge or show a connection to. If you find that they love hiking, for example, send them an interesting, related article. You can send books, photos, tickets, and more. Be creative but not in a creepy stalker kind of way!

I know a guy. It worked in the movie *2 Guns*, with Marky Mark and Denzel, why not you? Be that guy or gal who knows everybody. Get out. Get connected. Go to the hottest events. Know what's going on and who's doing what. Find a reason to connect with people whenever and wherever you can.

Cut humble pie out of your diet. You know you are the best, so practice saying it. Learn how to convey that you are a perfect fit for your audience and that you are uniquely qualified and the best choice to address them. Speak up for yourself. Do a lot of horn tootin' and be your own best source of PR.

Been there, done that. Showcase all your speaking experience. You don't have to be on a stage to deliver speeches and make presentations. Find an opportunity to practice public speaking every day, even if it's only to your cats, dogs, or kids. Speak to anyone or anything.

Be relevant and cutting edge. New and innovative ideas are sure to get people excited and engaged. But even if you don't have a new solution to an age-old problem, you can communicate and position yourself as relevant and important by carefully aligning what you say with the goals of your listeners. Help them feel that they are special and that you want them to be among the privileged few who get to experience the benefits of what you provide.

Put a stamp on it. Snail mail? Huh? What's that? While email is a convenient and super-easy way to fire off a quick message, people love getting real mail that is hand addressed directly to them. Send cards, letters, postcards, and packages to potential contacts. Focus your mailings on a common interest or goal and express your appreciation for their efforts and hard work. If you read that someone in your target area has been promoted or recognized for a special achievement or that someone has opened a new business, send a congratulatory note through the mail. When you meet, they will remember what you did.

CHAPTER 12

SELL WITH AUTHORITY

ove it? Hate it? There doesn't seem to be an in between. Closing the deal? *Love it*! Without question, we love to close deals. That's a no brainer. The more you close, the more money you make. You can sell all day long, but if you're not closing, you're out of business. You may not realize it, but you are selling constantly. Every single day you sell people on ideas. If you have kids, you are pitching to them endlessly. We sell our friends or spouses on which restaurant to go to or what movie to see. Whether you love it or hate it, you are doing it. So, why not do it with authority?

Selling is the key component to everything we do in business. I always say, "If you aren't selling, you aren't in business." You need to sell every day to generate ongoing, sustainable leads and revenue. It is paramount to business growth and expansion. If you are not a fan of selling, then it may be hard to do it well. People who dislike selling get frustrated and sometimes avoid selling all together. Some feel that selling is awkward, sleazy, and inauthentic. But the fact is, your success in business is directly proportional to your ability to sell: yourself, your services, and your ideas.

How do you sell with authority when you hate selling or even mildly dislike it? First, look at sales from a different perspective. Sales is about helping people. Every time you make a sale, you're helping a person experience the transformation they seek. Whether it's overcoming their challenges and problems, or realizing their hopes and aspirations, you make a meaningful impact in their lives with your selling. You're helping them get from where they are to where they want to be, all while creating the business you've always hoped for. So, tell me this: if sales is all about helping others, why do so many resist the sale?

For most people, the idea of selling conjures up the vision of a sleazy salesman in a polyester suit. No wonder selling makes us uncomfortable. Reframe the role of sales and its place within your business to get you excited about offering your gifts to the world. Reframing may not be easy, but ponder this analogy. If a person is drowning, going down for the third time, and you are a world-class, certified lifeguard, do you hesitate? Of course not! You know you have the skills and expertise to save the drowning individual. Or if you have expert training as a paramedic and you see someone bleeding to death, you will apply the tourniquet. You will use your skills without hesitation, because you know the victim needs it. It is a matter of life or death.

Life or death is an extreme, but your prospect just might feel that way about her business. Reframing is seeing sales from the buyer's perspective instead of your own. Put yourself in the shoes of your prospect, and you will see things differently. A great example of reframing is depicted in a scene from *Orange is the New Black*.[25] In Season 5, inmate Frieda has been locked in the kitchen pantry with some other inmates. During the riot, two correction officers are holding the inmates. While the others engage the guards, Frieda fashions a blow dart out of drinking straws and various kitchen supplies. She lands the darts perfectly and injects both guards. She cheerfully informs them that the darts have been laced with poison, and if they want her to whip up an antidote, they'd better let her out of the pantry. The guards struggle with the decision to free her but believe they will die if they don't. Naturally, they buy in!

Let me help you see sales differently. First, let's define *sales*:

1. the exchange of a commodity for money; the action of selling something
2. give or hand over (something) in exchange for money

3. persuade someone of the merits of

4. cause (someone) to become enthusiastic about

5. the act of selling; *specifically*: the transfer of ownership of and title to property from one person to another for a price

Now let's look at my sales definition for CODE to Close™: Sales is *closing* that results from a conversation between an expert (seller) and a person who needs what you offer (buyer). Selling is, first and foremost, a transaction between you (seller) and the prospective buyer or buyers (ideal client) where money is exchanged for goods or services. The sales conversation is the art of mastering the close by using active listening, open-ended questions, and authentic support.

Selling is simply offering your knowledge, expertise, and services to rescue another from his or her problem or dilemma. Never underestimate the level of pain or frustration your ideal client is experiencing. I am living proof that the pain of an unexpressed dream or vision can be deeply tormenting. I worked in a variety of industries for years, and I was miserable. I wanted so much more, but I had no idea how to even begin to do what I truly wanted to do in the world. I wanted to be a speaker and a trainer or coach. I didn't have a clue how to turn this into a real paying career for myself. I would cry on my way to work because I hated working for someone else. And I cried on my way home because I was afraid of never being able to replace the money this position offered me. I was stuck and frustrated. No one knew the depth of my misery except me.

One day, as I browsed my computer for new adventures, an email arrived in my inbox. The subject read, "Do you want to be a life coach?" I opened it and immediately felt a wave of hope. The email answered all my questions about being a coach. I clicked *yes* and found myself on a call with a coach. She asked all the right questions, and I got all the right answers. The opportunity offered everything I needed, and it was a perfect fit. I was all in! I was "sold." I knew the program was the vehicle to take me where I wanted to go: freedom. During that conversation, I never felt taken advantage of or tricked into buying. I felt understood.

I invested in myself. Your buyer will make an investment when she says yes. The sales process is not about creating a buyer. It is about helping the buyer determine if you can solve her problem. You are helping her make a decision about her future that is beneficial for her and for you. She says yes to herself because you foster her courage to do so. For sales conversations that convert, use your INTROmercial™ effectively and often. Deliver your INTROmercial™ in 17.5 seconds to capture the attention of your ideal buyer. In addition, deliver your big-impact, big-income talk with the Speak to Profit formula from any platform. These lead generation tools pave an easy path to the buying and selling process.

The focus of sales is on prospects and what's in it for them. Base your sales process on the specific buying style of your prospect. After over thirty years of selling both products and services, I have created a C.O.R.E. Code to Close system that will help you convert clients easily and quickly.

C.O.R.E. CODE TO CLOSE

Who are you?

Who are you at your core?

How are you selling to others?

How does who you are at your core affect closing the deal?

Your answers to these very important questions will help you to close with ease. It is imperative to own and recognize *why me* and *why now*, no matter the cost. Your C.O.R.E. Code to Close consists of your characteristics, competencies, and values. Your innate skills and genius to close with confidence require a clear understanding of who you are selling to and what it takes to get to their *yes*. In an earlier chapter, you identified your values. Now, let's look at your characteristics and core competencies.

Characteristic, as defined by Dictionary.com

char·ac·ter·is·tic ˌke(ə)ktəˈristik/noun

plural noun: **characteristics**

a feature or quality belonging typically to a person, place, or thing and serving to identify it. "inherited characteristics"

Synonyms; attribute, feature, quality, essential quality, property, trait, aspect, element, facet; mannerism, habit, custom, idiosyncrasy, peculiarity, quirk, oddity, foible . . .

Make a list of your key characteristics for a deeper understanding of yourself. We will use these characteristics to further understand how you operate throughout the sales process. Knowing your characteristics, as well as your core competencies and values, will boost your confidence and conversion.

core com·pe·ten·cy; as defined by Dictionary.com
Noun plural noun: core competencies
a defining capability or advantage that distinguishes an enterprise from its competitors.
a defined level of competence in a particular job or academic program.

Wikipedia: "A core competency results from a specific set of skills or production techniques that deliver additional value to the customer. These enable an organization to access a wide variety of markets."

Basically, your core competencies are what you do best. What are you so good at that no one else can even come close? Maybe you have the ability to develop and communicate to others how you can support them. Maybe you provide motivation and support, enhance others' commitments to their goals or visions, build or maintain relationships, or convey confidence in others' ability to be successful, especially at challenging new tasks. Maybe you are innovative and creative. Your ability to identify your skills and talents will accelerate your sales success.

According to Collins Dictionary, the definition of *code* is, "The genetic code of a person, animal or plant is the information contained in DNA which determines the structure and function of cells, and the inherited characteristics of all living things." We each have a code by which we live. By nature, we are drawn to what is most like us. Think about your school years. To fit in, you sought out your people, gang, or group of peers. These friends aligned with who you are and how you show up in the world. You had similar characteristics and things in common. We look for sameness. I've heard this craving or need for sameness referred to as coding.

Berit Brogaard, Director of the Brogaard Lab for Multisensory Research at the University of Miami, published a *Psychology Today* article entitled, "Are We Attracted to People Who Look Like Us?" Brogaard's educational background includes a medical degree in neuroscience and a doctorate in philosophy. Her article demonstrates how your C.O.R.E. Code to Close is an instrumental component to your success. According to research reported in the July 2010 issue of the *Personality and Social Psychology Bulletin*, we are attracted to people who resemble our parents or *ourselves*. I have noticed this in the world of selling, and it is a primary reason people cannot close the deal. Their capacity to sell is limited to a pool of prospects who are most like themselves. Is this true in your sales experience? It's great to sell to those like you, but how many people in the marketplace fall into that category? With limited prospects, your sales will cap and you won't exceed your income goals. The solution is to expand your ability to sell to the masses by knowing your C.O.R.E. Code to Close.

First, let's explore why you are attracted to people who are most like you. One reason is you're awesome—that's for sure. Another reason is they speak your language. Your C.O.R.E. Code to Close will help you expand your ability to speak multiple buying languages.

YOUR C.O.R.E. CODE TO CLOSE™

In my sales career, I've experienced, trained, and coached many different types of individuals who provide valuable products and services. Each individual falls into one of four main sales styles:

C: Catalyst
O: Optimizer
R: Relationship Builder
E: Expert

These styles represent a combination of characteristics, competencies, and values. A deeper look into the C.O.R.E. Codes will help you understand not only how you operate in the sales conversation, but how you can effectively communicate with the buyer. Let's look at these styles one at a time. While doing so, you can use the information to assess which of the four main styles is most like you.

C: CATALYST

The Catalyst takes action. When the Catalyst has a good idea, he is fully invested in starting now and moving to success. The Catalyst is competitive and influences others to move. The Catalyst finds thrill in the pursuit (the hunt) of the sale or the prospect. He loves the challenge. First and foremost, he's driven to bring a prospect to *yes*, not only because he cares about the sale, but because he believes people should act on their ideas. The Catalyst is fast on his feet and generates more solutions in seconds than others do in a lifetime. He is skillful at recognizing the need and matching the buy. The Catalyst is one of the stronger performers in sales. The Catalyst expertly convinces the prospect to buy a service or product based on the outcome and benefits, without going into depth about the features. He is inspirational and elicits courage and trust from his prospects. When it comes to money, he is a master negotiator.

The Catalyst leaves money on the table by over inspiring and motivating the wrong buyers. He sells to people who aren't a good fit for his products or services. The Catalyst experiences a consistent flow of people who have buyer's remorse, and he ends up having to resell them even after they buy. His buyers often pay late or go into default. Catalysts are often short on follow-up and can be impatient in the rapport-building arena. He goes from zero to sixty in no time and leave his prospects in the dust.

Catalysts exhibit the following *primary traits*:

Troubleshooting	Enjoyable	Acclamation
Negotiating	Improvising	Trending the Latest
Storytelling	Refinement	Styles
Achievement	Courageous	Affluent
Flexibility	Sporting Designer	Contest Takers
Captivating	Labels	Charismatic
Strategizing	Practicality	Stimulating
Mediating	Amusement	Showmanship
Problem Solving	Driving Luxury Autos	Celebratory
Competitive	Appreciate Aesthetics	Spontaneity
Ambitious	Passionate	Newness
Respond to Crisis	Adventurous	
Create Teams	Great Starters	

The Catalyst can be described as having the following *primary dislikes*:

Discontentment	Confinement
Management	Defeat
Borders	Quiet
Finances	Long-Term Planning
Time Limits	Preparedness
Specifics	Duplication
Directions	Habitual Routines
Jobs	Orders

Agendas

Administrative Work

Busybodies

Time Cards

Superfluous Gatherings

Delays

Details

Scheduled Work Hours

The Catalyst can be described as having the following *primary behaviors:*

Entrepreneurial in spirit and behavior

Performs gracefully in sports and the arts

Positive, but struggles with blind faith

Prefers concrete ideas and useful theory

Dislikes waiting and gets bored easily

Functions best through hands-on learning

Loves beauty and anything aesthetically pleasing

Skillful at negotiation

Opposes rules, routine, and structure

Seeks out and chases opportunity

Takes risks to achieve goals

Looks at more productive ways of doing things

Gets more done that others in a fraction of the time

Combats boredom with extra risk

Solves a problem quickly by ignoring the rules and others' expectations

The Catalyst gets it done!

O: OPTIMIZER

The Optimizer is one of the most loyal of the codes. She is skillful at presenting the offer with structure and careful planning. The Optimizer will deliver a systematic presentation that follows a logical pattern from A to Z. She is detailed and highly formal in sales conversations. She helps the prospect fully understand the features of the service or product and how they will be delivered. She is on time and dressed professionally, whether in person or virtually. The Optimizer has straightforward, no-frills facts and data to substantiate her results to meet the prospect's needs. She is conscientious of budgets and will never be too pushy on the close.

The Optimizer leaves money on the table by describing too many features. She overloads her prospects with details and fails to connect on a personal level. She focuses on the facts and not on the emotional aspect of the deal. She fails to color outside the lines and is not flexible to meet the needs of the prospect. The Optimizer sees negotiation as a set system or plan rather than a spontaneous style of conversation. She can be set in her ways and in the plan, and she loses the deal due to an inability to see it from the client's perspective. To the Optimizer, it makes sense to keep things in order and on task.

The Optimizer can be described as having the following *primary traits*:

Duty

Financial Planning

Responsibility

Uniformity

Gives Instruction

Controlling

Gives Concessions

Earnestness

Rulemaking

Loyalty

Clear Objectives

Security

Insurance

Honesty

List maker

Dependability

Structured

Coordinator

Dedicated

Systems Oriented

Excellence

Established Outcomes

Reliability

Pattern maker

Orderly

Accomplished

Logistical

The Optimizer can be described as having the following *primary dislikes*:

Inconsistency

Lack of Focus

Change

Disarray

Disorder

Insecurity

Liability

Setbacks

Wasting Time

Misrepresentation

Foolishness

Interference

Condemnation

Paying Interest

Excessive Spending

Taking Chances

Antics

Squirrel Syndrome

Rebels

Surprises

Delays

Confusion

Instability

Misuse

Missing Deadlines

Risk

The Optimizer can be described as having the following *primary behaviors*:

Prefers both time-tested and proven establishments

Not fond of people who question their authority

Expects honest behavior from others

Strive to maintain order and security in her environment

Leads agenda-driven meetings that are efficient and timely

Has a black-and-white view of the world

Establishes and implements functional systems

Follows all tasks through to completion

Values heritage

Works well with systems, routines, and procedures

Expects everyone to follow established rules

Is committed to truth and clear standards

R: RELATIONSHIP BUILDER

The Relationship Builder is warm and friendly, asking questions and showing interest in his prospects. He makes every effort to connect on an emotional level with a prospective client. Many Relationship Builders naturally see great results with this type of selling because they instinctively know and truly understand what their prospects need. The Relationship Builder is dedicated to the best interest of the prospect and makes sure that the product or service is a very good fit. If you have this Code, you will genuinely connect and display interest and concern. The Relationship Builder will carry out the relationship beyond the initial connection. He is attentive in his follow-up, and follow-through is important to this Code. The Relationship Builder maintains the same level of interest in his prospects, whether they buy or not.

The Relationship Builder leaves money on the table by being too darn nice and timid. He doesn't want to offend anyone, and he tends to be too empathetic towards objections. I have known the Relationship Builder to nurse a relationship for a year before asking for business. Four million coffees later, he gets a *no*! This style is generally very heart-centered, and money isn't his favorite subject. The downfall of this Code in closing is that he waits for the prospect to offer the sale. This is an injustice to the prospect because it puts an unfair responsibility on someone who looks to hire you for support—not the other way around.

The Relationship Builder can be described as having the following *primary traits*:

Fosters a Good Cause

Consensual

Genuineness

Philanthropic

Loves Kids

Advocacy

Tactfulness

Empathy

XOXO's

Fairness

Inspirational

Makes Direct Eye Contact

Trustworthiness

Embraces Fellowship

Family Focus

Partnership

Focus

Service

Idea Generator

Intimacy

Affection

Positive Disposition

Unity

Makes Referrals

Loyalty

Physical Gesturing

Compassion

The Relationship Builder can be described as having the following *primary dislikes*:

Intimidation

Seclusion

Deceitfulness

Tyrants

Discord

Disingenuousness

Selfishness

Self-Pride

Failure

Blackmail

Deception

Gluttony

Misconduct

Hypocrisy

Fabrication

Greed

Solitude

Fraud

Pragmatism

Politics

Disrespect

Unfair Selling

Tactics

Stress

Prejudice

The Relationship Builder can be described as having the following *primary behaviors*:

Always supportive and empowering of others

Feels disdain toward those who are not true to themselves

Supports others in reaching their potential

Dislikes those who focus on material possessions

Demonstrates enthusiasm and passion in his endeavors

Tends to avert confrontation and competition

Is on a quest for self-actualization and wants others to do the same

Shows appreciation easily and in many ways

Trains, motivates, and counsels people in need

Thrives on interaction with people, individually and in groups

Lends a helping hand wherever needed

Demonstrates resiliency during hardship

E: EXPERT

The Expert prefers a more logical and less emotional approach, demanding of herself the task of becoming expert in anything and everything related to her industry, product, and service. She positions herself as a problem solver, able to answer any question and tackle any issue that the prospect presents. The Expert is sometimes affectionately referred to as a *know-it-all*. And, frankly, she is. She has ample relevant information and keeps up with latest trends and changes in technology, strategies, and reports. Once the prospect realizes what a great resource the Expert is, he fully trusts her knowledge and accuracy. The Expert will demonstrate her knowledge and expertise through facts, charts, and diagrams.

The Expert leaves money on the table by making the mistake of not asking enough questions. She matches prospects with the best product for their needs, but she doesn't connect with them in a more personal way. There is little relationship building and far too much conversation about features and technical concerns. This may be because the Expert doesn't feel as comfortable with people as she does with her product and services. The Expert will benefit by remembering that, no matter the sales situation, whether for an individual or organization, people buy based on emotion first and information second. When people feel a connection, they unconsciously strive to work with you. The Expert can be too shy on heart and too heavy on logic.

The Expert can be described as having the following *primary traits*:

Analytical	Good Associate Reviews
Planning	Revelatory
Consumer Accounts	Knowledgeable
Diagramming	Puzzle Solver
Solid Credentials	Studier
Specialist	Applications
Evidence Gathering	Strategy
Fact-finding	Report Writer
Mathematical Equations	Technology
Electronic Devices	Satire
Higher Education	Originality
Instruction	Charisma
Variation	Degree Holder
Rationale	Sees the Big Picture
Outliner	

The Expert can be described as having the following *primary dislikes*:

Mechanics	Ineptitude
Suggestions	Insufficient Information
Sweeping Statements	Schmoozing
Revelry	Poor Listeners
Spectacles	Public Speaking
Meaningless Talk	Practicality
Emotions	Acknowledgement
Hype	Role Playing
Exorbitant Adoration	Short cuts
Enthusiasm	Social Gossip
Inexperience	Social Gatherings

Conjecture

Idiocy

Touch

Blind Ambition

Uncorroborated Claims

The Expert can be described as having the following *primary behaviors*:

Places heavy focus on the future and long-term results

Easily comprehends abstract ideas

Dislikes memorization without clear comprehension

Places high trust in logic and reasoning above all else

Prefers to resolve conflict logically and rationally while avoiding emotions

Shares and explains abstract ideas using diagrams and models

Self-critical and will discover errors before others do

Lays out map, plans, and accompanying strategies

Capable of focusing on several issues at the same time

Speaks with precision and easily hears contradictions.

Seeks out substantive conversation and dislikes small talk

Displays strong self-discipline

I hope you have identified your C.O.R.E. Code. You will likely have one dominant C.O.R.E. Code and other secondary codes. The C.O.R.E. Code traits, dislikes, and behaviors will also help you to recognize and identify not only your own but, your prospect's. This will help know his or her buying style. The sales conversation is far more successful when you are able to speak to the C.O.R.E. Code of your buyer.

The basic sales conversation format will remain the same. The words within that conversation will change according to the Code of your buyer. I have a very basic outline of the sales conversation, whether in person or virtually. I am not a fan of lengthy scripts that take the person from hello into dark pain and suffering and then close the deal on them. I do not believe that people buy in complete pain. In my opinion, the best sale includes a *yes* from a place of power. Powerful decisions come from information, awareness, and understanding. It is your job to make your prospects aware of their pain or problem and help them clearly understand your solution. In every sales situation, I ask these three questions:

1. What is working?
2. What is not working?
3. What would you love to be working?

Straightforward. I want to establish a partnership that results in a win-win, whether they buy or not. Keep in mind that your goal is to C.O.N.N.E.C.T., and you will be way ahead of the curve in sales. Here is what it means to C.O.N.N.E.C.T.:

C: Connect
O: Open
N: Needs
N: New Possibilities
E: Enroll
C: Coach
T: Take Action

COMPONENTS OF C.O.N.N.E.C.T.

The most important factor in the Connect Sales System is that your prospects need you more than you need them! Sell for their reasons, not for your own. Let's take the C.O.N.N.E.C.T. elements one at a time:

C: Connect. First and foremost, express appreciation for your audience or prospect's attention. Remember, you are looking for a fit, not a sale. You are qualifying them, and you are positioning yourself as the expert. It is a two-way conversation: they are listening for a solution, and you are listening for the match. Build rapport so that you will be the trusted advisor they hire. Validate and reflect what you hear from them and help them elaborate. "Tell me more." "Paint a picture of that for me." "What might that look like?" "How does that show up in your life or business?" "Are there other examples of that?" Focus on emotional involvement to determine the wants and needs of your buyer.

O: Open. Make them aware of their pain or problem and that they want or need a change. Ask leading questions to help them pinpoint the problem. "Exactly what have you tried?" "Exactly what isn't working?" "What is that costing you in your life/business/health?" Some people will not want to reveal their pain points. They will want to focus on what's working in your area of expertise. Call them on it. "It sounds like everything is working for you, so why did you want to talk to me?" This is where you need to spend the most time. Demonstrating the gap between where they are and where they want to be is a service to them because it helps them step into awareness and then make a decision.

N: Needs. Review their needs and assess what fits for them as a customer or client. Determine if you can help. "What I heard was _____." "I see two areas where you feel stuck." Reflect the pain or problem, validate where they are, and entice them to where they could be. Selling with authority means making your prospects aware of the problem and bridging the gap between their pain and the solution they desire. The bridge consists of all the benefits they will reap as a result of buying from you. Some people never make the offer, and others try to shortcut the sales conversation, skipping right to the offer without describing any benefits or value to their potential client. A prospect once said to me, "I've experienced many sales conversations. You are one of the first people to offer me some insights into my business instead of skipping straight to a sales pitch. Thank you."

Position yourself as the expert, position their pain, and bridge the gap by outlining the benefits you offer and how those benefits relate to where they are and where they want to be. Selling with authority means being of service to your prospects and helping them say yes to themselves, their dreams, or their business.

N: New Possibilities. What is possible for your prospect This is your opportunity to offer a vision of what could be. Help them imagine the next success they will experience when they implement your solutions and resources. Paint a detailed picture, so they can visualize, think about, and feel the potential results. Help them grasp the difference this will make for them. Let them draw their own conclusions.

E: Enroll. Bridge the gap between pain and desire. "To make this work, I would love to introduce an additional resource." Ask pivoting questions. "Do you have enough information to make a decision?" "On a scale from one to ten, how ready are you?" Determine how committed they are and how badly they want it. If the answer is six or above, move to the invitation or the offer. For anything less than that, go back to the Open step. They are not yet fully aware of the pain. People don't buy when they feel great and don't have a need in the world. They listen to you for insight that hasn't occurred to them. Ask, "With all that I have shared, does this look like something that will meet your needs?" More motivated individuals will count on you to actually tell them what you recommend. Make the appropriate suggestion with permission but be sure they make a decision. Always tie the benefits back to the pain and the possibility for the prospect's specific outcome. Bring value! It's important not to disclose the price until you have a *yes*. Price should never be the deciding factor for the buyer to purchase your product or service. The *yes* must be based on the value and benefits only. A *yes* based on price does not build strong business relationships, and it compromises loyalty. A *no* should be based on a genuine lack of need for what you offer, not price. Disclosing your price too soon breeds objections before you can demonstrate you have the solution they seek.

C: Coach. Let the benefits do all the work. Tie the benefits to the prospect's pain. This will help them accept the offer. *Be prepared.* This is where objections arise. They will claim no money, no time, or no deal. We will address overcoming objects, but the best focus at this point is to review the pain points and clarify what it's costing them right now to remain where they are. Use your previous experience and your sense of what they seek to answer their concerns.

I use phone conversations to enroll new clients if I am not speaking from a stage or presenting from a platform. In the early days of my business, I was very enthusiastic about helping people; I tried to solve all my prospects' problems on that initial call. In fact, I was so helpful that they loved me and would feel great relief just talking to me. But relief is not a solution to the prospect's problem.

There's no way I could fully solve all their problems on a single forty-five-minute call. In addition, when I solved their immediate problem, they would then be confused about the right next steps to take.

By trying to solve all their problems in one call, my conversations—and my sales process—grew longer and longer, costing me time and money and doing my clients a disservice. Why? When your potential clients ask you to solve the problem on the call, it's usually because they have needed help for quite some time. When you provide temporary relief, they are less likely to buy. So, give value and coach tehm through the buying process, not through their issue or pain. Don't give away the farm.

T: Take Action. Bob Proctor says, "Decision is the one mental maneuver that will change the trajectory of your life." Ask your prospects if they want to move forward. Let them decide either way, yes or no. Assure them you support either decision. Sometimes the decision is *not now*. If so, leave the door open for a follow-up connection. If they are a yes, put them into immediate action.

C.O.N.N.E.C.T. moves you through the conversation with the right focus: the buyer. If you can't solve a problem, you don't have a sale. Most people or organizations buy in an attempt to solve a problem or eliminate a pain. Many sellers spend too much time on the features and how they will be delivered rather than assuring the buyer that the product will solve the problem. Instead, focus on how your product or service can solve the three most critical problems your client is experiencing.

Use a script, if you need it, until you are confident with your delivery, but be very careful not to be plagued by what I call *script-itis*. The sales conversation is an organically evolving interaction. I have known people to spend hours creating presentations or scripts only to become so dependent upon them that they disconnect from the buyer and the buying signals. Successful selling, and more importantly, closing is dependent upon the level of connection you have with the prospect. Sometimes scripts keep you from being yourself, and you end up asking close-ended questions. Closing the sale requires the buyer to open up. Closed-ended questions result in missed opportunities to build trust. You limit the level of connection by playing it safe or asking leading questions or following the script. Many people try to lead buyers to say *yes,* rather than asking open-ended questions that will naturally take them to their own *yes.*

Your primary focus should be on the buyer, but please don't forget to ask for the deal. The effort of a sales conversation is wasted if you don't ask for the deal. The worst thing you can do is avoid closing the sale. Fear is the most common reason for failing to close—fear of rejection, doing it wrong, or violating the trust of the prospect. Know that these are your own fears and that not asking for the deal is a disservice to your potential buyer.

Selling with authority is the path you lead others to so that they are inspired, take action, follow through, and say yes to themselves. You cannot and should not deny your potential clients the opportunity to work with you now that they've sampled your expertise in the sales conversation and have come to trust you as an authority in your industry.

Selling can be scary and frustrating, and it can bring you to tears. I have cried more times after a sales conversation than I'd like to admit. In 1989, I started cold calling for Stivers Temporary Personnel. I was scared to death. I had to walk into large corporations and get past the gatekeeper to the decision maker. I got no after no. There were signs on every office door: "No soliciting!" And behind every door was the stern, unfriendly receptionist waiting to turn me away. I was just out of college and had no self-esteem. Every rejection devastated me. I learned very quickly that I needed to dodge these rejections and get through the door to the decision makers.

My first step was to identify my beliefs, stories, and feelings around selling. I hated selling but was desperate to make a go of it. Like many other people who think they don't like sales, I perceived selling as slippery, like a bait and switch. To be successful at sales, I needed to reframe the sales process and empower myself to understand selling my products and services as a responsibility, not a bait and switch or something I was "doing to others."

Remember, the sales enrollment process is an invitation. You're offering something valuable, whether it be a product or a service. If you don't give others the opportunity to buy and invest in themselves, then you're not serving the people who need you, and you're not serving your own purpose and gifts. Look, people have needs, and you just might be the solution to those needs. The only way to link the need with the solution is to invite prospective clients to buy. You can't offer you and your services for free. People buy emotionally and decide rationally. Until people invest, they will not listen to you. Free gets them nothing and gets you nowhere.

Also, people are not buying the steps, programs, products, or systems you have. They are buying you and the result they anticipate. This means you need to identify your prospects, and then you need to approach them in a way that speaks to their buying Code.

CODE THE SALE

I have encountered a number of selling styles in the past three decades, including slimy sales pitches and manipulative offers. I am not a fan of these selling styles. The way to sell with integrity is to sell authentically with authority. The prospect's best interest is always your priority. To sell with authenticity and authority, you need to understand *who* you are talking to in the sales conversation. Not who as in Bob or Denise, but who as in what is his or her C.O.R.E. Code? Learn how to code the sale, which means knowing the buyer's code (Catalyst, Optimizer, Relationship Builder, or Expert) through simple questions and a few easy observations.

Coding the sale helps you determine what makes your prospect tick and how to customize your sales approach to get a faster commitment to yes.

Coding the sale is an easy-to-implement, comprehensive sales connection and communication system. I have established this coding system to help you identify the key triggers to help your prospect say yes in a fraction of the time. I love immediate gratification, and I want results yesterday or the day before. Can you guess my C.O.R.E. Code? The coding system comes naturally to me, and I have developed it over the years through thousands of sales conversations. I believe that I was born to sell—anything. My father was a District Sales Manager in the world of engineering and nuclear power. My oldest brother sold software and software solutions. My other brother was in the world of hydraulics, selling to customers like Universal Studios. He sold the hydraulics for the *Jaws* amusement ride. My sister created a multi-million-dollar medical supply business. My other sister pushes ice cream and owns three Dairy Queens. If you think ice cream sells itself, think again. She is a master at coding her customers and has generated millions of dollars and millions of Blizzards. I pull up the rear, the youngest sibling who has learned from each one of them.

You do not have to come from a family of sales professionals and entrepreneurs. The coding system will help you shorten the life of the sale and increase your conversion ratio. When you discover key insights into your client's thinking, you will love selling. You will quickly connect on a deeper level with your prospects. You will fully understand their needs and know how to present the solution by clearly and effectively communicating in any situation. It is vital to know your prospects, speak their language, and move them into action, preferably a *yes*! Let's explore how to cut the time it takes to qualify your buyers, discover their unique buying language, and close the deal.

CODE YOUR BUYER

A number of telltale signs identify each Code. Notice what people wear, what they drive, how they greet others, and the way they maintain their office, desk, or car. Notice the people you connect with and observe the signs for each Code. Here are some things to notice that identify a prospect's C.O.R.E Code.

C: CATALYST

Characteristics of the Catalyst include:

- Motto: Fire, ready, aim
- Phone apps include photo editors, music, Offer-Up, YouTube, Uber
- Full of life and energy
- Center of attention, attracts attention with confidence
- Drives high-end, expensive car
- Dresses to impress, usually sporting designer labels that standing out
- Seizes the moment and is the first to volunteer or jump in
- Loves discussing and acting on new ideas
- Easy-going, fun loving, spontaneous, and gregarious
- Charming, popular, and friendly, makes new friends easily
- Active, team player, encourages others to participate
- Cares not what others think of her
- Gets straight to the point and calls it like she sees it
- Loves a good debate
- Does what is to be done rather than talking about what might be
- Adrenaline junky, moves at her own pace, which is *fast*
- Antsy; sitting is the bane of her existence
- Greeting: high five

O: OPTIMIZER

Characteristics of the Optimizer include:

- Motto: Ready, aim, fire

- Phone apps include budget, maps, productivity, to-do lists, project planning, financial
- List maker and goal setter
- Polished and professionally dressed
- Conservative, formal, and traditional
- On time for everything
- Often refers to budget or money
- Drives economy car
- Leads and organizes groups by implementing systems; plans quickly
- Highly organized in both office and social surroundings, color coding and sizing
- Takes things literally, follows the rules, and respects boundaries to the letter
- Model citizen, upholds the mission of an organization and society
- Finishes every task, project, or goal
- Averse to and avoids chaos and unpredictability; appears stiff and unapproachable
- Keeps others on task
- Wallet, purse, money, files, car, and clothes are organized
- Greeting: Handshake, potentially cupping with the other hand

R: RELATIONSHIP BUILDER

Characteristics of the Relationship Builder include:

- Motto: Ready, are you ready, are we all ready, let's go
- Phone apps include Pandora, Plant Nanny, art and design, affirmations, family, friends
- Wears flowing, comfortable clothes
- Hugger, close talker, toucher, lover
- Friendly, warm, connects with the masses

- Happy, cheerful, thoughtful, lends a hand
- Idealist, looks for good in all
- Strives to please everyone in the group and the world
- Loves a mission or cause and inspires others to join
- First person to help without being asked
- Maintains eye contact and touches while talking with others
- Avoids debates and heated conversations
- Rescues anyone who appears in need and defends the weak in a group
- Not highly organized
- Open-minded and flexible, goes with the flow, as long as it is for the good of all
- Bumper stickers: COEXIST, World Peace, Baby on Board
- Greeting: Hug

E: EXPERT

Characteristics of the Expert include:

- Motto: Aim, get ready to get ready to get ready, aim some more, then fire
- Phone apps include books, sci-fi, business, news, education, high tech, puzzles, games
- Organized mess in his surroundings, knows exactly where everything is piled
- Pocket or purse filled with latest devices and gadgets
- Appears to be the know-it-all and enjoys sharing it
- Researches everything
- Low tolerance for lazy, shortsighted individuals who are focused on their own needs
- Methodical decision maker, because everything is based on intellect
- Makes blanket statements

- Challenges the status quo
- Makes definitive statements and opinions about how things should be
- Drives a high-tech vehicle
- Conversations are challenging and feel like a debate
- Word nerds, point out every typo or grammatical error
- High-level tech talk
- Quiet, reserved, observer, stand-offish; deep in thought
- Greeting: Handshake

QUESTIONS TO CODE THE BUYER

The right questions can streamline the sales conversation and accelerate the close. The following questions will help you narrow down the prospect's code and speak her language. Make no mistake, this is not a trick or manipulation to get the sale; it is the best way to honor the thinking and decision-making process of the prospect.

For example, I code high as a Catalyst. I take action fast and get results. I have been known to come up with the idea for a program or product, and before it is even created, I have sold ten of them. I have very little patience for details and data, just get to the bottom-line. I bought a Toyota 4Runner Limited—"limited" because that is important to a Catalyst. I also drive a Lexus, F150 SuperCrew Limited, and I used to drive BMWs. As a Catalyst, it is important to me to have the best, no matter the brand. I walked into the dealership and met with the Fleet Manager. Why? The Fleet Manager is able to give a better deal than the retail sales person. A good deal speaks to the Optimizer Code in me. The rep started off our conversation by showing me pictures of his newly adopted son and vacation photos. If we were having a friendly dinner that would be great, but I was buying a car, and I buy in Catalyst mode. I know what I want, and I will move on the right decision quickly. We literally spent thirty minutes in the getting-to-know-you phase of the sales conversation. I kindly interrupted and said that I would love to hear about his family on a test-drive. I outlined the rest of the sales process for him. It was pretty straight-forward: test-drive, negotiate or not, done. We did just that, and in record time I was driving my new SUV.

Can you guess what I did next? I coached him on C.O.R.E Code selling and asked him to introduce me to the person who is responsible for dealership training. Success! I met the manager of the dealership and landed a training opportunity. A Catalyst, like me, loves a challenge and loves navigating a win.

For me, every conversation is an opportunity to ask for a referral, sale, or introduction. The best way to take advantage of every interaction is to use your unique INTROmercial™ to open the conversation about what you do and then code your prospect. On my revisit to the doctor after having minor surgery, I began talking about what I do and sharing my INTROmercial™. The doctor informed me his practice had a sales team that could use some support. Every encounter has the potential to be a closed deal. Use the tools in this book and make it a habit to sell through your messaging. It works.

You can ask a variety of questions to code your prospects. When you question your prospect, you are looking for *types* of answers, not specific answers. Listen for a common theme that shows up throughout the interaction. The theme of the Catalyst will be action, doing, results, risk, thrills, and urgency. The theme of the Optimizer will be strategy, order, routine, thinking, and discipline. The theme of the Relationship Builder will be feeling, service, helping, visions, dreams, and connection. The theme of the Expert will be intellect, thinking, facts, proof, and logic. Keep the C.O.R.E. Code descriptions handy while you are on a sales call. Here are some sample opening questions to help you know your buyer, along with a few C.O.R.E. Code answers to get you started. Watch for the common theme of each answer.

QUESTION: TELL ME A BIT ABOUT YOURSELF.

C: Will relay a list of accomplishments and information.

O: Will start with what they do, for how long, where they live, and basic personal data.

R: Will tell you everything and will ask about you.

E: Will respond with a clarifying question: "What would you like to know?"

QUESTION: HOW DID YOU GET STARTED IN THE WORK YOU DO?

C: It was an exciting idea, a new challenge to overcome, an opportunity. I fell into it. I loved the competition.

O: I applied my skills and systems to the current market trend. It made sense.

R: It's been my dream, my passion. I love it; it was a good cause. It was my chance to help others.

E: I have the degree, the knowledge, the vision, and an innovative solution. It was a logical fit.

QUESTION: HOW DO YOU SPEND YOUR SPARE TIME?

C: Activities, concerts, festivals, outdoors, competition, parties, test driving a Tesla.

O: Discount shopping, organizing, cleaning, purposeful, small-group conversations.

R: Family, meditation, spiritual activities, nature, friends, connections, supporting a movement.

E: Reading, internet perusing, researching, sci-fi events, Tech Talk, puzzles, drones.

QUESTION: WHAT ASPECT OF YOUR JOB DO YOU ENJOY THE MOST?

C: Doing, implementation, action, achievement, being the best, generating ideas.

O: Budgeting, accounting, organizing, creating systems, project planning, spreadsheets.

R: Serving customers/clients, collaboration, counseling, coaching, support, retreats.

E: Research and development, big picture, technical support, innovation, software.

QUESTION: WHAT TASKS OR ASPECTS OF YOUR WORK DO YOU DISLIKE OR AVOID?

C: Paperwork, numbers, details, repetitive tasks, office work, content creation, research and development.

O: Sales, networking, small talk, collaboration, building relationships, doing video.

R: Closing the sale, cold calls, research, details, micromanagement, analysis, collections.

E: Celebrations, sales, rapport building, recording video, networking, getting out in public.

QUESTION: IF YOU COULD MEET ANYONE YOU CHOOSE, PAST OR PRESENT, WHO WOULD IT BE AND WHY?

(*Why* will help you further identify their code. For example, the Relationship Builder will want to meet with Oprah Winfrey for her charitable work, and the Optimizer will want to talk about business strategies.)

C: Michael Jordan, Oprah Winfrey, Danica Patrick, Emmitt Smith, Tony Robbins.

O: Suze Orman, Barack Obama, Alan Greenspan, George Washington, Colin Powell.

R: Mother Teresa, Gandhi, Jesus, Michelle Obama, Eleanor Roosevelt.

E: Albert Einstein, Bill Nye (the Science Guy), Bill Gates, Steve Jobs, Stephen Hawking.

THREE QUESTIONS I ASK IN EVERY SALES SITUATION

1. What's working?
2. What's not working?

3. What would you love to have work?

Here are the most frequent responses to these three questions:

QUESTION: WHAT'S WORKING?

C: Generating leads, great ideas, putting everything into action.

O: Having a plan, being fully aware of numbers, systems being in place.

R: Providing and delivering wonderful support products and services.

E: Automation in place; certifications achieved; solid, proven content or product.

QUESTION: WHAT'S NOT WORKING?

C: Not closing, too many leads to follow up on, tired of hearing no, no systems at all.

O: Not closing, no leads, not getting out enough, too much time spent on systems.

R: Not closing, charging too little, inconsistent message, afraid to sell, number avoidance.

E: Not closing, technical message, hates sales, not enough ideal clients out there.

QUESTION: WHAT WOULD YOU LOVE TO HAVE WORK?

C: Systems and delegation of follow-up tasks, administrative work, and organization.

O: Step-by-step sales script or system that helps to gain more exposure and clients.

R: Eliminate fear of sales, closing, and money. Confidence in asking for the sale.

E: Get comfortable selling out in the world and hone in on a clear message.

DEALING WITH OBJECTIONS

Nothing is more defeating and annoying than an objection. You have built a rapport with the prospect, you coded her, fully understand her needs, and then, just when you think it's a done deal, she says no. What? Why? It makes no sense. She loved you and what you had to offer. I hate when I get a no, not because I won't be able to pay my bills, but because I know the prospect genuinely would benefit from my support. Okay, truth be told, I also hate the word *no* because sometimes I take it personally. I know it isn't about me, but I let my feelings get in the way, and it hurts.

In my early twenties, I started cold calling in the employment industry. I called on corporations and small businesses to help them staff their organizations. I walked in hoping to get past the gatekeeper at the front desk. I ignored *no soliciting* signs and the *skull-and-crossbones* warning sign for sales reps. I faced rejection numerous times every day. I was sensitive, I hated the rejection, and I hated the no. During one cold call to Wendy's Corporation, the front-desk employee was direct and barked, "Get out!"

Tears welled up in my eyes. I began to cry and promptly turned to leave as the door opened in front of me. I wanted out of there as fast as possible. A very nice gentlemen asked me if I was okay. I sucked it in enough to say yes. He stopped me from exiting and asked if he could help me. I said I was there to meet with the Human Resources Department but was told to get out. The man handed me his card and escorted me back to his office. He was the President of the Midwestern Division of Wendy's International. I learned a great lesson that day, *cry!* No, seriously, I learned that I can survive a *no* and that it isn't about me. I learned that the receptionist was a temporary employee from another service, and they were looking to replace her. Guess who got the order? Yes, indeed, me!

On another occasion, I walked into an office, and the reception looked up in anger and annoyance. I promptly said, "Damn sales people!" She was shocked by my introduction and apologized, disclosing that she'd had a bad day.

You don't know the whole story when you get a nasty look, a hang up, or a no. It's easy to make up a story about what is wrong with you, your product, or your service. The sales conversation helps you discover the whole story behind the objection.

People spend endless hours crafting and perfecting their pitch without a second thought to the objections that will come afterwards. Some degree of resistance, uncertainty, or a flat-out objection to your offer is inevitable. If you ineffectively handle these objections, you lose the sale. I don't know about you, but I grew tired of losing deals to responses like, "Your price is too high," "Now isn't a good time," or, "I don't have the money." So, I set up a system for overcoming objections. You might hope your prospects won't object, but they always will. Why not spend some time preparing for them in advance?

Handling objections means responding to the buyer in a way that helps them gain clarity, confidence, and proof that will alleviate their concerns or resistance. There are three different kinds of *no* in sales, each with its own challenges. *No* can mean: "You haven't provided enough value," "Not yet," or, "I'm not interested." Each no requires a different response, so the art of selling requires you to differentiate between rejections and a need for further clarification.

People will defend their objections. Even if you attempt to convince the prospect she shouldn't think or feel this way, the reality is that she does, and it is your job to help her fully realize her pain or problem and understand that you have the solution. Be careful not to pressure her into backing down. Convincing is not an effective way to overcome an objection. Coercion creates a stronger no, and even worse, you begin to lose trust and the rapport you've established. Help her come to a different conclusion of her own accord by using empathy, reflection, understanding, and open-ended questions. You will further discern if she is a fit for your product or service throughout the objection process. If you are working harder than she is to get to *yes*, it is not a fit.

There is a difference between a sales objection and a brush-off. Objections are authentic statements and a way for prospects to gain greater understanding of themselves and what you have to offer. A brush-off is an indirect way of saying, "No, I see the value in your product or service, I love it, but I can't figure out a way to commit because of X." A brush-off translates to, "I am out but can't say no." Work through a brush-off by asking directly, "If it weren't for the time or money, would you buy?" If the answer is no, pack it up. End the call by appreciating her honesty and wishing her the best of luck. I usually will ask for a referral at that time. Word to the wise, a pain-in-the-butt prospect usually will refer another pain-in-the-butt. Beware.

In my experience, true objections are simply excuses to disguise fear. Find out the whole story and support the buyer through it. The prospect may have a fear of failure, wasting money or time, going over budget, not getting a return on the investment, unworthiness, decision making, or risk. Objections are based on the buyer's sense of worthiness and belief in herself enough to invest in her future.

My all-time best sales tip is that you will never overcome an objection you agree with. You examined your money story early on to be constantly aware when it comes up. Objections trigger your money story and can interfere with overcoming the client's no. Awareness is the best prevention for killing a deal. Your response to most objections will reflect your patterns around money and finances, your money story. Also, the way you have overcome objections in the past was based on your C.O.R.E. Code. Unconsciously, no matter what, you addressed objections with your Code. For example, an Optimizer would attempt to overcome objections by giving more information about features, deliverables, and proven plans. If an Optimizer is dealing with a Relationship Builder, he will get nowhere. The Catalyst will be long gone at that point. The Expert will want proof and evidence of your credentials and experience.

Dealing with objections is an art form. Each step in this book has prepared you to speak with confidence and sell with authority. Speaking with confidence puts you in the position to sell. Now it's time to close. Everyone can sell, but they can't always close. My goal is to get you closing the deal more often and in less time. How? By navigating objections using a very simple coding system. Shall we?

I will demonstrate some strategies for overcoming objections using the C.O.R.E Code to Close system. I will highlight the common theme for your response to each Code. You will work with the theme rather than the exact script. I'll begin by outlining the theme for each C.O.R.E. Code to help you effectively overcome any objection.

> **C: Catalyst.** Always address the wins they will experience as a result of working with you and, more importantly, how quickly and easily they can expect these results. Provide the opportunity to act now. Catalysts are always on the go, and you must prove that you will not slow them down. Details are boring and unnecessary. When Catalysts decide, they go with their gut feeling. They are used to moving fast, so do not give them the opportunity to think about it. Their goal is to be the best, outpace the competition, and make that happen in their own way. Shortcuts are vital to Catalysts, and action is their

primary operating procedure. So, give them bottom-line information, cut to the chase, stay away from rules and accountability, and challenge them to say yes to themselves.

O: Optimizer. Always emphasize systems, structures, strategies, tracking, and goals. Be accurate with your information and never exaggerate. Never use a hype line like "10 times your business." Demonstrate stability in your business, be organized, and be on time. Emphasize the proven success of your formula, product, or service. Most things make sense if they are in sequential steps. Be organized in your delivery of your features and benefits. Alleviate any risk and talk about guarantees, if you provide them. The Optimizer will be your most loyal and faithful client or customer.

R: Relationship Builder. Use words like *support, partner, community, serve, help,* and *together.* The Relationship Builder will respond to authenticity and good counsel and will trust that you are keeping their best interest at heart. Feeling words are great ways to connect with the Relationship Builder. Never use any pressure sales tactics, manipulation, or outrageous claims of what they can do. They are not a fan of big dollar signs. The Relationship Builder is all about serving the greater good. Focus to relieve the sales tension during the conversation by asking how they feel. Check in often, ask how they're doing, what they're feeling, and how you can best support them in their decision. Emphasize that you will include them in your community and partner with their success.

E: Expert. Always provide proof, proof, and more proof. This can be social proof, testimonials, statistics, numbers, and credentials. If you have a degree, accreditation, or certification, share that information. Offer Experts connection with some of your past clients, so they can get validation of your work. Experts love information and details. The Expert is the one Code that almost always needs to think about it. They are not fast to make decisions, but when they do, they make the right decision. It is important that Experts know you are aware of their brilliance, degrees, successes, and knowledge.

Use these sample questions to discover some general information and what is most important to your prospective client. These questions will help you prepare to overcome objections.

- What would you like to see in this situation?
- If you could wave a magic wand, what would you like to have happen?
- What outcomes are you looking for?
- On a scale of one to ten, how committed are you to making this change?
- What is it costing you to stay where you are?
- How committed are you?
- Are you more committed to the past than to the possibility?
- Are you going to let doubt interfere with your commitment?
- Why do you think you haven't succeeded?

COMMON OBJECTIONS

Here are some common objections and how to address each Code when navigating their objections. You can use the scripts word for word but be sure your delivery is natural and authentic. I can apply these scripts to anything I sell. For the purpose of this book, I will share my own business sales examples.

OBJECTION: "I DON'T HAVE THE TIME."

I love this objection, because it is the easiest one to overcome. First and foremost, make sure you are pitching to your prospect's priorities. If what you have to offer truly will not support his goal, then you need to understand that clearly. Uncover what's really going on. Determine his situation and customize your approach based on his needs. In many cases, that requires digging deeper to discover what's most important for him. He may not understand how what you offer can benefit him. Review the benefits as they relate to the specific pain he expresses.

Depending upon the person and our rapport, I might say, "Well, then, thank goodness you and I are talking. Get your credit card, you truly need me. If you don't have the time to build your business quickly and easily, then you can't *not* work with me." No matter the person's Code, this works, because every Code desperately seeks more freedom to do what they love.

Here are some codified responses to the *no time* objection:

> **Catalyst**: "What I know to be true is you are a person who takes *action*. Unfortunately, it may not be the right action. You stay busy, but do you always generate income? My program offers you a way to take right action and free up time to *have more fun*, rather than working harder and not smarter. I work with people to do, in half the time, what others take months to do."

> **Optimizer**: "My greatest concern is that your *systems and strategies* are not properly designed according to your business *plan* and desired outcome. What I offer will allow you to set up the right systems for the right outcomes.

In addition, I will help you with revenue generating *sequential steps* that make sense and get *consistent* results. My structure is based on *proven formulas.*"

Relationship Builder: "Everyone gets the same number of hours in each day. It may not always *feel* that way, but the reality is if you don't have time, you need to invest in a system of *support and partner* with me to do things in new way. Bottom line, you serve more when you have a *community* to *stand with you* in your work. Tell me more about what you are doing, and let's see if I can *support* you in your *mission.*"

Expert: "I know you have the *knowledge, experience, degrees, and tools* to create the income you have projected. With more than *thirty years* of sales training and professional speaking, and having created *two multi-million-dollar* companies, I know this will work for you. I have closed *five and six figures* from stage using my Speak to Profit formula. With your *experience and credibility*, we can get your work out in the world."

OBJECTION: "I DON'T HAVE THE MONEY, AND I CAN'T AFFORD YOUR FEES."

This is the most common objection. If you address this early on, it is much easier to overcome later in the conversation. Ask this question early in the conversation, when they share with you what is not working for them. "What is it costing you to be in this situation?" The cost doesn't have to be financial. It may be costing them peace of mind, relationship with family, future opportunity, etc.

When a prospect says your product or service is too expensive, it isn't always about price. They may have the money or budget for your product, but you haven't demonstrated enough value to justify your price. Or it isn't about price or value at all, it is a way to hide the real concerns. When you hear the pricing objection, find out what's the deeper reason.

My standard response to the money objection is, "I get that a lot, and what I find to be true is money is a great reason, but not always the real reason. What might be the real reason? Sometimes it is about not getting the return on your investment. Other times, it has more to do with your belief in your ability to get the results you need. Money should not be the reason not to invest in yourself. If you really can't put food on the table, I completely understand, and we should not move forward. But if you are masking a fear, let's look at that. If money really is the issue but you are *all in,* let's go find the money." No matter the Code, I approach money casually and with a curious mind. I never hear it as a firm no, until they say no.

> **Catalyst**: "I am confused, you said you wanted to make over a hundred thousand dollars this year, yet you are *hesitating* to take the *action* necessary to make that happen. You are not one to sit around and hope for results, you are a *catalyst* to put things into *action* and get *results*. This program is not for those who won't get moving. This is for people like you, who want the *shortcut* to closing more deals and *fast* results."

> **Optimizer**: "Where is it? You know how to *save* the money, and more importantly, get the money. Let's see how we can make this happen for you and *honor the budget* you have set up this year. The best part of our working together is you will increase the *income line item* and create a bigger *savings account*. And I have a variety of *payment plans* that you can choose from to make it fit."

Relationship Builder: "Let's look at how *we* might find the money together to get you the *support* you need. In absence of a *support* structure, you end up in the world of entrepreneurship *alone* and without a *community of like-minded people* to hold you up when you need it. In this program, you will be *connecting* with others who experience the same thing you do at varying levels. Let's *partner* in making this happen."

Expert: "I've seen *brilliant*—almost *too smart*—individuals like you let their thinking get in the way. *Hesitation* comes from overthinking and worrying it to death. I get it. Let me help you find what you need to make an *informed decision*. What information do you need to make an *educated decision*? With more than *thirty years* of sales training and professional speaking, and having created *two multi-million-dollar* companies, I know this will work for you. I have closed *five and six figures* from stage using my Speak to Profit formula. In addition, I have worked with clients starting at your exact stage, and both have *accomplished* [state outcomes, testimonials, facts, statistics]. Would you like to talk to them? I would hate for you to base your decision on money/cost rather than on the results or the *big picture*."

OBJECTION: "I AM NOT SURE THAT YOU CAN HELP."

Catalyst: "Fair enough. Share with me when you haven't put things into *action* and gotten the results you set out to *accomplish*. It might feel like a *challenge* to you now, but when I give you the easy steps, you will *hit the ground running*. You will have the information you need to *do it* *your way* and *do it now*. I have seen this work for people who take forever to get started. Imagine what it will do for you!"

Optimizer: "I can understand that, but this program offers *solid systems* and fits perfectly into what you have set forth in your *plan*. *Incorporating* this program is the *next logical step* in the *advancement* and *growth* of your brand and business."

Relationship Builder: "This is not the first time I have heard this comment. *I get it*. The key to my work with clients is *partnership*. I don't let you wander into the world trying to figure all this out. I walk with you. Heck, *we become so close* I may show up for the holidays. You will *lean* on me and allow me to *believe* when you aren't able to believe in yourself. I will *support* you and *guide* you all the way. I never let anyone *fall through the cracks*. I am *here for you,* and I am *fully invested* in your results, happiness, and *fulfillment*."

Expert: "I am sorry, but that is the farthest thing from the *truth* in my opinion. You are *smart* and *know* exactly what you are *capable* of in this market place. Let me lend you my *experience, knowledge, and success* over more than thirty years to develop your INTROmercial™, talk, and closing techniques to give you the direction and discipline to grow your business consistently. My *extensive* experience resulted in the creation of *two multi-million-dollar* companies, and I know this will work for you. I have closed *five and six figures* from stage using my Speak to Profit formula. I never waste anyone's time, and I get results."

OBJECTION: "I HAVE TO THINK ABOUT IT."

This is the worst objection ever! It's not a *no*, exactly, but it's not an objection you can work with or overcome. The real work here is to make your prospect reveal the real reason for needing to think about it. Do some digging with direct statements or questions to get more information and know your right next steps in the conversation. The only Code who needs to think about it is the Expert. The Expert will think and think again. Patience is vital when closing an Expert. The responses for the C, O, and R are interchangeable with a few theme adjustments.

> **Catalyst**: "What is there to think about? If you have to think about it, I have not done my job explaining how this fits for you. Successful people make decisions, and they make them *quickly*. Thinking about it is the last thing you need to do. You expressed your goals, and the only way to *accomplish* them is to *act*. Help me understand what might really be getting in your way. You are not a *think about it* person."

> **Optimizer**: "What is there to think about? If you have to think about it, I have not done my job explaining how this fits for you. Let me *detail* for you the *structure* of my program and the *projected* outcome of each *step* you will take. My *proven track record* will show you the *reliability* of my program and formulas. After turning profits around by 240%, I think my program is a *fit* for what you want to accomplish."

> **Relationship Builder**: "I am so sorry. The fact that you have to think about it is an indication that I have not done my job explaining how this fits for you. *Help me understand* your need to think about it. I would love to *support* you in making the right decision. My work in the

world is to provide the *best support*, whether you work with me or not. I know *thinking about it* usually is an indication of fear or doubt. What might it be for you?"

Expert: "Excellent. *How long* would you like to think about it? I know you need time, but I don't want to go too long, because *thinking* is what has put you behind on your timeline. What *information* can I provide that will help you *think* about it over the next few days?"

The *think about it* objection requires a bit more attention. It's common when they feel they need more time to consider the pros and cons. Unfortunately, when you give them more time, fear kicks in. Fear will convince them they don't really need your program, product, or service. Here are some good questions to ask:

- What do you need to think about? If you go away and think about it, I won't be there to answer your questions, so let's tackle them right now.
- What might you be afraid of? I'm going to give you everything you need to reach your goal. What is missing for you?
- In that case, let's go over any obstacles that might come up when you are thinking about it, so I can support you in what might be stopping you from getting what you want.

If you can't get them past this objection, then set up a follow-up appointment in two to three days. Do not let them leave without setting a time. If they won't set another appointment, you must dig for the true objection. I confront the no-appointment situation by asking more defining questions. Sometimes, I am even so bold as to say, "That's interesting. You say you are very interested, yet you don't want to set up a time to revisit the conversation. In my experience, this is a no. If it is a no, let me coach you for a minute. Making definitive statements in your business, like yes and no, is a vital component of your success. If you are unable to say no to me, I can tell you exactly why you aren't closing the deal. So, can we get to the real answer? Are you a no? Or is it something else?"

This always flushes out the truth, and I can navigate the next objection and bring them to a decision. The best approach is an honest, gentle confrontation.

OBJECTION: "I HAVE TO TALK TO MY SPOUSE/ BUSINESS PARTNER ABOUT IT."

This objection could be a strategy they use to avoid giving you an answer. However, there are some great approaches you can use to clarify for yourself and for them the help you can offer. Prevent this objection by asking early in the conversation how they operate in their business and if they are the sole decision maker. Sometimes, the prospect makes all the decisions and does all the work but is financed by a spouse, partner, or other. They may not disclose this to you until it comes down to the money portion of the conversation.

Approach this objection as it unfolds. They will give you clues to the next step according to how they answer probing questions. You will encounter spouses and partners who are employees and who don't think like a small business owner or entrepreneur. Employees and entrepreneurs have a different understanding of business, so be proactive and coach them through the presentation to their spouse or partner.

Catalyst: "Oh, this *could take some time*. What is the best way to make a decision *now* and still honor the relationship? To further understand, is your spouse in business with you? Who generally makes the financial decisions? What do you think your spouse will say about this?"

Optimizer: "Is your spouse your investor? In other words, is he or she paying the bills while you are building your business? If so, let's make sure you are *investing in the right strategies.*"

Relationship Builder: "What about setting up a call *for the three of us*, so I can explain things?" Or, "Let me role play with you to *support* you when you have the conversation. It is important to me to *honor* your relationship."

Expert: Experts will *never* use this objection. They are the Experts, and they know what they need to do. They trust their own capacity to decide.

Objections are inevitable. No matter their Code, you can use any and all of these responses for prospects. During the conversation, use your best judgment and be flexible with your responses. You will code the buyer and respond accordingly. Buyers hire coaches to help them improve on their weaknesses. I am a high Catalyst. People hire me to be direct and action oriented, but I have to speak their language in order to close and honor them throughout the coaching relationship.

Being proactive is important to prevent a slew of objections. The greatest benefit of the Speak to Profit formula is that it helps you overcome a high percentage of objections as you deliver your talk. This streamlines the sales conversation and puts the focus on when, not why. Another way to proactively prevent objections is to give value early in the sales conversation, but do not solve their problem. Providing relief through coaching works against the sales process and closing the deal. You might be tempted to solve the problem because you know what needs to be done. Do not coach them or comment about how they can fix it. Relief comes from your prospects investing in themselves and taking a stance for their success. You can also seed prior to the sales conversation and within the sales conversation. Share experiences from your previous clients. Include statistics, surveys, or testimonials.

Objections offer you the chance to help and support the buyer. This is the time to show off your success, brilliance, and genius. Sell with confidence in order to close the deal. Be direct, be firm, and be of service. Most of all, be you.

CONCLUSION

peak with confidence and sell with authority! It isn't always easy, but it is simple. Whether you have been speaking and selling for years or you are just getting started, delivering a powerful talk that sells is the easiest and fastest way to catapult your success. I previously mentioned my client Heidi Mount. Her story merits repeating in greater detail. When I met Heidi, she displayed glossophobic tendencies. The thought of speaking reduced her to tears and panic. Heidi didn't believe in herself. She believed that if she got anywhere near a stage, she would die. I enrolled Heidi in my SuperStar Mastery program, which included speaking and sales training. Heidi was convinced she was a lost cause. Nothing could be farther from the truth.

I've mentioned before that I grew up in a complicated family. I felt invisible growing up. I did my best not to shine, and I had no self-esteem whatsoever. I never imagined that I would stand on stages (big or small) speaking about myself and my work in the world. That's why I knew with all my heart that, with my support, Heidi's would be a Cinderella story. I promised her that, for the first six months, I would never mention the word *stage* to her. Our goal was to get her in front of her ideal audience without her dropping dead.

Heidi works in the dental industry and knew that she could appear on a number of podcasts and radio stations. Her first assignment was to get booked using her INTROmercial™. In less than a week, she was booked on a huge podcast to tens of thousands of dentists. I witnessed her interview firsthand. All I could think was *poor Heidi*. I'm not sure, but it appeared she cried at one point in the interview. She froze a handful of times and occasionally lost her way, but she forged ahead and completed the interview. When I received her call later that evening, I thought it would be a 911 rescue mission call.

"I sucked, didn't I?" Heidi asked.

"Yes, you did suck, but it was your first," I said, trying to console her. But then she surprised me.

"Jane," she said, "I sucked so bad that I landed an $18,000 client as a result of the interview!"

The following week, Heidi got another $6,000 contract from someone listening to that podcast. Oh, to suck so terribly! Many would kill for a bad talk that paid out like that one.

Speaking and selling is an inside-out job. It requires a strong belief in yourself, your product or service, and the ability to articulate your message with clarity and confidence. Your past will always be with you. Patterns, beliefs, and stories don't just go away. Be aware of how you think and what you believe. Each day, navigate the thoughts that run through your mind and give them a voice. Express yourself in every area of your life, so you can take a stand for what you do and what you know. Own your point of view. The journey of success is not about the amount of money you accumulate. It's not about how many sales you convert, your degree of fame, or being the best. Success is simply about your true desire—a desire driven not by your ego, but by your heart.

I measure success by the amount of love I can take in and give out, and by how much peace and satisfaction I can experience. My ego motivates me on my journey to success; my heart keeps me focused on what is important. You have a *why*. Why do you do what you do? Get to the heart of what matters in your life and success by asking why again and again. Knowing your *why* keeps you aligned with your core values, your mission, and your fulfillment.

My goal is for you to step fully into your power, find your voice, and deliver a message that helps the masses. My goal is for you to speak with confidence and sell with authority. You deserve it!

NOTES

1   Amy Cuddy, "Your Body Language May Shape Who You Are." Lecture, TED Global, Eidenburgh, Scotland, June 27, 2012.

2   Ralph Waldo Emerson, *Self-Reliance* (White Plains, NY: Peter Pauper Press, 1967).

3   Dr. Pauline R. Clance and Suzanne A. Imes, "The Imposter Phenomenon in High Achieving Women: Dynamics and Therapeutic Intervention," *Psychotherapy Theory: Research & Practice* 15, no. 3 (1978): 241-247.

4   Maya Angelou, accessed March 29, 2018, https://www.goodreads.com/quotes/220406-each-time-i-write-a-book-every-time-i-face.

5   Genevieve Behrend, *Your Invisible Power* (Bottom of the Hill Publishing, 2010).

6   *Groundhog Day*, directed by Harold Ramis, (1993; Los Angeles, CA: Columbia Pictures).

7   Saul McLeod, "Pavlov's Dogs," accessed March 29, 2018, https://www.simplypsychology.org/pavlov.html.

8   Gay Hendricks, *The Big Leap* (New York: HarperCollins Publishers, 2009).

9   Nelson Mandela, accessed March 29, 2018, http://azquotes.com/quote/185315.

10   Ralph Waldo Emerson, accessed March 29, 2018, http://azquotes.com/quote/544116.

11   Rhonda Byrne, *The Secret* (New York: Atria Publishing Group, 2006).

12   Napoleon Hill, *Think and Grow Rich* (United Kingdom: Capstone Publishing LTD, 2009).

13   Greg Flaxman and Lisa Flook, PhD, "Brief Summary of Mindfulness Research," accessed March 29, 2018, http://marc.ucla.edu/

workfiles/pdfs/marc-mindfulness-research-summary.pdf.

14   Raymond Holliwell, *Working with the Law* (Arizona: LifeSuccess Productions, 2004), 67.

15   Wallace Wattles, *The Science of Getting Rich* (Massachusetts: Elizabeth Towne, 1910).

16   Dr. David Isner, "'Givers Gain' Is a Standard, Not a Sword," accessed April 12, 2018, http://ivanmisner.com/givers-gain-is-a-standard-not-a-sword/.

17   Nelson Mandela, accessed March 29, 2018, https://azquotes.com/quote/185309.

18   Neale Donald Walsh, *Conversations with God: An Uncommon Dialogue* (Massachusetts: Hampton Roads Publishing Company, 1995), 22.

19   Garrett Ray Harriman, "A Brief History of Anxiety & Fear," accessed March 29, 2018, https://explorable.com/e/history-of-anxiety-and-fear.

20   John O'Donohue, accessed April 12, 2018, https://www.goodreads.com/quotes/94019-the-ego-is-the-false-self-born-out-of-fear-and.

21   Bob Proctor, "Proctor Gallagher Institute: Decision Making," accessed March 29, 2018, https://www.proctorgallagherinstitute.com/tips-and-tools/decision-making.

22   Robert Fulghum, *All I Really Need to Know I Learned in Kindergarten* (Illinois: Dramatic Publishing Company, 1999), 8.

23   Chet Holmes, *The Ultimate Sales Machine: Turbocharge Your Business with Relentless Focus on 12 Key Strategies* (New York: Penguin Group, 2007).

24   Yogi Berra, accessed March 29, 20181973, https://www.brainyquote.com/quotes/yogi_berra_110034.

25   *Orange is the New Black*, season 5, episode 2, "F*ck, Marry, Frieda," directed by Constantine Makris, written by Jordan Harrison, aired June 2017, on Showtime.

WORK WITH ME IN PERSON

I am excited that you've read *Speak with Confidence. Sell with Authority.* Now you have the knowledge to find your voice in business, command any stage, and increase your sales!

With over thirty years of sales and speaking experience, I've learned a great deal about turning your message to money and closing the sale. Since you've read my book, I'd love to work with you in person. I can guide you to apply what you've learned to your business and overcome any blocks keeping you from closing more deals and taking more stages.

Every year I hold a live, three-day event called, ***Let's Talk Impact***. Guess what? You're invited! At *Let's Talk Impact*, I work with you to create an authentic message that screams YOU and shows why you are the go-to expert in your field.

You will also . . .

- Find out more about how to monetize your message and close the room from any platform.
- Practice coding your buyers so you can authentically communicate with them in their language and overcome any objection that's keeping them from fulfilling their dreams.
- Create and refine your own unique INTROmercial™.

- Network with other like-minded business professionals.
- Have a ton of fun and much more!

To get your ticket, go to
JaneMPowers.com/lets-talk-impact

To stay in touch with me, visit my locations online:

- JaneMPowers.com/author
- www.facebook.com/JaneMPowers
- www.linkedin.com/in/Jane-M-Powers/

You can find a short video introducing each chapter of my book when you visit my website or read the eBook version of *Speak with Confidence. Sell with Authority.* I hope the videos will be a quick way for you to get valuable content and easily share my message and information with other people who could benefit.

Thanks again for taking the time to read my book. Let me know what you think! I'd love to hear from you.

Stay amazing,